Dear Amber —
    May this little book
answer some important
questions for you!
                    All my love,
                        mimo
                            ü

TOUGH

Questions About

THE BIBLE

TOUGH
Questions About
THE BIBLE

JOEL R. BEEKE

CF4•K

Thanks to Paul Smalley and Ray Lanning for their assistance on this book
- Joel Beeke.

Scripture quotations are taken from the King James Version of the Bible.

10 9 8 7 6 5 4 3 2

Copyright © 2013 Joel R. Beeke

ISBN 978-1-78191-230-0

First published in 2013 and reprinted with
Truth For Life,
P.O. Box 398000, Cleveland,
Ohio 44139, U.S.A.
www.truthforlife.org
by
Christian Focus Publications Ltd.,
Geanies House, Fearn, Tain, Ross-shire,
IV20 1TW, Scotland, U.K.
www.christianfocus.com

Cover design by Daniel van Straaten
Printed in the U.S.A.

CONTENTS

Tough
Questions About
The Bible

1. How do you know that God is real? Prove it!

We can know that God is real by using our eyes, our minds, and our hearts. Our *eyes* see His glory in the world around us (Ps. 19:1), so big and yet carefully designed that it can't be the result of a big explosion. How did the earth get precisely where it needs to be so that it's not too hot or too cold for us to live on it? We see His glory in our bodies with their intricately shaped parts which could not come from chemical accidents (Ps. 139:14). How did your body come together so that every one of your 300 trillion cells is made of tiny molecular machines each doing its job right on time? Romans 1:20 says, "For the invisible things of him from the creation of the world are clearly seen, being understood by the things that are made, even his eternal power and Godhead; so that they are without excuse."

Our *minds* tell us that God is real because we know there is right and wrong and that one day we will be called to account for our actions. This is called conscience. Romans 2:14-15 says, "For when the Gentiles, which have not the law, do by nature the things contained in the law, these, having not the law, are a law unto themselves: which shew the work of the law written in their hearts, their conscience also bearing witness, and their thoughts the mean while accusing or else excusing one another."

If there were no God to command us and judge us, then there would be no right and wrong, only the law of the jungle where anyone can do whatever he wants. But our consciences tell us otherwise, especially when others wrong us. The best way to know that God is real is with our *hearts* as we read the Bible and hear Christ speaking to us through it. Jesus called Himself the Good Shepherd and said in John 10:3, "The sheep hear his voice: and he calleth his own sheep by name, and leadeth them out." True Christians know that the Lord is real in a way that goes beyond observations and arguments. They have heard the Shepherd's voice, and they know Him personally. God is real to His people in a way that is inseparable from the Bible but beyond explanation, for He lives within His children.

2. How did we get the Bible?

God spoke His Word to people, then God helped them to write it down, and then God led His church to collect their writings into one book. Hebrews 1:1-2a says, "God, who at sundry times and in divers manners spake in time past unto the fathers by the prophets, hath in these last days spoken unto us by his Son."

God spoke to prophets such as Adam, Enoch, Noah, and Abraham from the beginning of time. Among the first written words from God were the Ten Commandments, written by the Lord Himself on tablets of stone (Exod. 24:12; 31:18; 34:1, 28). God also commissioned Moses to write history, law, and prophecy (Exod. 17:14; 24:4; 34:27; Deut. 31:9, 19). As centuries passed other prophets also wrote down what God revealed to them (Isa. 30:8; Hab. 2:2).

The people of God recognized that these books were from God, and collected them into what we call the Old Testament. At the time they were written on scrolls, long rolls of leather, parchment, or papyrus, an early form of paper. They were written in the Hebrew language (with a few parts in Aramaic). About a hundred and fifty years before Jesus was born, these books were translated into Greek, because that language was spoken in much of the known world.

When Christ came, He gave apostles and prophets to His church to lay the foundation of New Testament truth as the Holy Spirit revealed it to them (Eph. 2:20; 3:5; 4:11). Some of them wrote histories of what Christ and His apostles said and did (the Gospels and Acts); others wrote letters to other Christians and churches (Epistles and Revelation). Christ and His apostles also recognized the Old Testament books as the true Word of God (Matt. 5:17-19; 2 Tim. 3:16-17).

Again, the church recognized that these new writings were not the wisdom of men but the Word of God and collected them as the New Testament. They were written in Greek. Over time, the scroll was replaced by the codex, the kind of book we know today, with pages sewn or glued to a binding with covers.

The church for a long time used a Latin translation of the Bible called the Vulgate. Later Martin Luther translated the Bible from Greek and Hebrew into German, Jacques LeFevre d'Etaples into French, and William Tyndale into English. Tyndale's work became the basis of the King James or Authorized Version, which was published in 1611.

What an amazing book the Bible is! Under the inspiration and guidance of the Holy Spirit, its many books, written by dozens of authors over a span of 1,500 years, were collected and preserved through centuries of persecution and neglect, and finally, translated into our own language. Yet they speak to us today with fullness of truth, life and power, because they are the Word of God, which shall stand for ever (Isa. 40:8).

3. Why is it so important to follow the Bible? Doesn't everybody have their own opinion?

The Bible is the Word of God; it cannot be broken (John 10:35). When God speaks, we must listen (Amos 3:8). We dare not add to it nor subtract from it (Prov. 30:5-6). When men contradict the Bible, we must obey God and not men (Acts 5:29).

When Martin Luther was summoned to go to the city of Worms in 1521, he knew that he would face great opposition and danger. His preaching of the Bible had made him a lot of enemies. Emperor Charles V was no friend of the Reformation. Luther might be burned at the stake. When the officials of the government and the church asked him to take back what he had taught and preached, he asked for time to think and pray.

The next day the court came together again. Luther declared that he could not take back what he said unless they showed him from the Bible that he was wrong. He said, "Unless I am convinced by testimonies of the Scriptures or by clear arguments that I am in error—for popes and councils have often erred and contradicted themselves—I cannot withdraw, for I am subject to the Scriptures I have quoted; my conscience is captive to the Word of God. It is unsafe and dangerous to do anything against one's conscience. Here I stand; I cannot do otherwise. God help me! Amen."

The Bible alone has God's authority to bind our conscience. We cannot build our faith on man's opinions. We must stand on what God has spoken, even to the death.

4. What is the Apocrypha?

The word apocrypha means "hidden things." It is a collection of thirteen books written by Jews after the Old Testament was completed but before Jesus Christ came. They included histories of the Jewish people, stories about people and angels, and sayings of the wise.

The Roman Catholic Church teaches that the Apocrypha is part of the Bible and should be revered as the Word of God. However, the apocryphal books were never part of the Hebrew Old Testament. Nor did Jesus quote from them as the Word of God, as He did from the law, prophets, and psalms of the Old Testament (Luke 24:44). For this reason, Protestant churches do not count them as part of the Bible.

These books give us some idea of what Jews believed in the period between 300 and 100 B.C. They contain some interesting history and ideas, but they are not the Word of God. They teach false ideas such as praying for the dead and suffering in purgatory before going to heaven—ideas contrary to the true Scriptures.

5. Why are some words colored red in the Bible?

Some Bibles put the words of Jesus in red. But the Greek manuscripts of the New Testament don't use a special color. People didn't start printing red-letter Bibles until 1899.

Red-letter Bibles are trying to show how important Jesus is as our prophet and teacher. God once said about Jesus, "This is my beloved Son, in whom I am well pleased; hear ye him" (Matt. 17:5). If anyone will not listen to Christ, then God will punish him (Acts 3:22-23).

The red color is also a reminder that God's covenant comes to us through Christ's blood (Luke 22:20). Only by His blood shed on the cross for our sins can the promises of God be ours. If we trust in His blood for salvation from our sins, then God is our God and we are His people.

There is one danger in printing Jesus' words in red. Some people might think that those words are more important than the rest of the Bible. We must remember that the whole Bible is really God's Word. The prophets spoke and wrote down the exact words that God gave them (Jer. 1:9; 36:1-2, 6). Paul wrote, "All scripture is given by inspiration of God" (2 Tim. 3:16), which means it was spoken forth by God's Spirit.

Peter said that the Word of God is "a light that shineth in a dark place," and explained that it is very important for us to know, "No prophecy of the scripture is of any private interpretation. For the prophecy came not in old time by the will of man: but holy men of God spake as they were moved by the Holy Ghost" (2 Pet. 1:19-21).

So whether the words are black or red, remember that whenever you read the Bible or hear it preached, Jesus Christ is speaking to you.

6. Does the Bible contain a secret code? How do we decode it?

Some people have gotten very excited about secret messages that their computers have supposedly found in the Bible. However, the Bible does not contain a secret code hidden in its pages. People who try to prove a "Bible code" could use their computers to find a code in anything, including this book. This does not please God, because it distracts people from paying attention to the plain message the Bible has for everyone who is open to hear it.

Sometimes people complain that the Bible is too hard to understand. And there are some things in the Bible that are "hard to be understood" (2 Pet. 3:16). That's why ministers and professors study the Bible very carefully, pray, and read and write books about Scripture known as commentaries.

But the most important messages of the Bible are clear. The Bible is not full of darkness, but is a light that shows us the way to go. Psalm 119:105 says, "Thy word is a lamp unto my feet, and a light unto my path." Even children who have learned how to read can understand much of the Bible and grow wise by it (2 Tim. 3:15). Psalm 119:130 says, "The entrance of thy words giveth light; it giveth understanding unto the simple."

How can you understand the Bible? Read it with diligence, working hard to hear what God is saying. People will work hard to learn about football with all its rules, teams, and players. Shouldn't we be willing to work hard to understand God's Word? Read through a book of the Bible from beginning to end, instead of skipping around. Otherwise it's like walking into the middle of a conversation and you don't know what they're talking about.

Whenever you open the Bible, remember that it is the Word of the great and all-powerful God. Read with reverence. Read with a desire to know God. Think about what you read. Try to see how it points to Christ, because Jesus said the whole Bible is about Him (Luke 24:44). Talk with other Christians about it, especially people who are wiser than you. Trust in Christ as He shows Himself to you. Don't just read the Bible; do what it says. Obey God's Word.

And always, always, pray for God to teach you. Psalm 119:18 gives us a good prayer to pray: "Open thou mine eyes, that I may behold wondrous things out of thy law." Pray for God to teach you by His Spirit, to give you understanding so that you can obey Him, to make you go in the right path, and to turn your heart away from this world and to His Word (Ps. 119:33-36).

7. How do you know what is true, biblical religion?

Biblical religion has the Bible as the foundation of its teachings and worship. We must always ask, "What has God said in His Word?", and not, "What does man think is good and wise?" For God is true, but men are corrupt liars (Ps. 58:3; Rom. 3:4). True religion does not worship God in ways that people made up, but offers to God what He commands.

The Heidelberg Catechism (Q. 2) does an excellent job telling us the core of biblical religion. It says that in order to "live and die happily" in the comfort of Jesus Christ it is necessary to know three things: 1. How great my sins and miseries are (1 Cor. 6:10-11; John 9:41; Rom. 3:10, 19); 2. How I may be delivered from all my sins and miseries (John 17:3); 3. How I shall express my gratitude to God for such deliverance (Eph. 5:8-10). These three things still stand as defining marks of true religion.

First, true religion deals honestly with the sad condition of fallen man. We must know ourselves as lost and needy sinners (Ps. 51). We must reject the lies that tell us to believe in ourselves and find our pride and joy in human accomplishments (Jer. 9:23; 17:5-6). If you want to find a true church, look for a congregation that will tell you that you are a hell-deserving sinner who must be saved from the wrath of God (Rom. 1:18; 2:5; 3:9-20).

Second, true religion teaches us that God saves sinners through Christ alone by a Spirit-worked faith. False religions, whether they call themselves Christian or not, make our salvation and happiness depend ultimately on man's works. But the good news of the Bible is that the Father sent the Son to redeem sinners, and the Father and the Son send the Spirit to apply that redemption to our lives (Gal. 1:4-5; 3:13-14; 4:4-6).

19

Biblical Christianity is centered on Jesus Christ, and glories in salvation by grace alone (Eph. 2:8-9; Phil. 3:3). Christ alone is our righteousness before God, and we are justified by faith alone, not our goodness (Gal. 2:16).

Third, true religion calls men to live for God in response to God's mercies in Christ. We must present all that we are and all that we have to God as a living sacrifice (Rom. 12:1). Even though it's popular to ignore God's laws, true Christians love the laws of their Lord (Ps. 119:97, 113-114, 163-165). They delight to obey the commandments of their Savior, even as they grieve over the sin that remains in them (John 14:15; Rom. 7:24-25). This is the life of freedom, for the Holy Spirit sets them free from sin and death (Rom. 8:2) to keep the perfect law of liberty (Ezek. 36:27; James 1:25).

Tough
Questions About
Sin and Sadness

8. Why did God make midges?

Well, we don't call them "midges" in the United States, but we too wonder why God made mosquitoes. For God created everything that exists (Gen. 1:1). I think the best answer is Genesis 1:30-31, "And to every beast of the earth, and to every fowl of the air, and to every thing that creepeth upon the earth, wherein there is life, I have given every green herb for meat: and it was so. And God saw every thing that he had made, and, behold, it was very good. And the evening and the morning were the sixth day."

This text teaches us that all of God's creation was very good when God completed it—including midges. But it also tells us that in the original creation animals and insects did not feed on flesh but on plants. So midges (and tigers for that matter) did not bite us. In God's perfect ecosystem, they probably helped to consume some of the vast produce of the plant world to keep it in check. So the annoying and sometimes dangerous bites of insects remind us of the horrible consequences of the fall.

This question leads into a discussion of sin and our need for a Savior. Westminster Shorter Catechism (Q. 19) says, "What is the misery of that estate whereinto man fell? All mankind by their fall lost communion with God, are under his wrath and curse, and so made liable to all the miseries of this life, to death itself, and to the pains of hell forever."

Sadly, all the miseries of this life includes midges, mosquitoes, and malaria. Happily, these miseries can serve to awaken us to the coming judgment, so that we flee to Jesus for refuge. We can put up with midges today if we know we will enjoy Christ forever.

9. What is the fall of man? When did it happen?

The fall of man does not mean falling down on the ground and hurting yourself. It was a spiritual fall from the happiness God put us in when He made us down to the sad state we are in today. We call it the fall because it was as if God had put us on a throne in the tower of a beautiful castle, but we threw ourselves off the tower down into the moat outside of the castle. The fall broke our bones and covered us with the disgusting slime of the moat. Now we cannot climb back up the wall or wash ourselves clean.

God made mankind, both man and woman, in His image (Gen. 1:26-27). We were like God. We were perfect in knowledge, holiness, and righteousness (Col. 3:10; Eph. 4:24). God made us the rulers of all the earth (Gen. 1:28; Ps. 8:4-8). He put the first man and woman in the paradise of the Garden of Eden, and gave them a commandment to keep. But they broke the commandment, and so sin and death came into the world (Gen. 2-3).

Adam, the father of the whole human race, stood as our representative before God. His sin brought death and damnation to all men, women, and children (Rom. 5:12, 18). Now we do not know God, seek God, love God, or do what is right (Rom. 3:9-18, 23). By nature, we are all sinners.

10. What is a sinner? What is sin? How do I know if I sin?

Sin is being, thinking, saying, or doing anything that displeases God. It's like shooting an arrow at a target and missing the mark but instead, hitting a rock and breaking the arrow. We know that we sin by God's laws, where He tells us what is right and wrong. "Sin is the transgression of the law" (1 John 3:4). God's Ten Commandments are like a mirror in which we can see how ugly our sins have made us. "By the law is the knowledge of sin" (Rom. 3:20).

A sinner is anyone who sins. Jesus said, "Whosoever committeth sin is the servant of sin" (John 8:34). Sin isn't just a mistake we make. Sin comes from our hearts (Mark 7:21-23). Our bad choices show that we have bad hearts (Matt. 12:33-35).

We need to understand that when the Ten Commandments tell us not to do bad things like murder or stealing, they are also telling us that it's sin even to want to do those things in our hearts. Christ said it is a great sin to be angry with someone and call him a bad name (Matt. 5:22). The Tenth Commandment tells us that even coveting is sin, like when you greedily want a toy or book or clothes and are not content and thankful with what you have.

11. How could God punish Adam over such a little thing as eating a piece of fruit?

When Adam and his wife took the fruit from the tree of the knowledge of good and evil, it was a very bad sin (Gen. 2:16-17; 3:1-6). It was not the fruit that made it so bad as what eating the fruit said about how they thought of God and how they treated Him.

First, God had generously given them every other tree in the garden to eat from. It was easy for them not to eat from just one tree when everything else was theirs. But to eat from it was to say, "God has not been good to us."

Second, God had commanded them not to eat of that one tree. To eat that fruit was to say, "I don't have to obey God. He's not my boss! He's not my Lord!"

Third, God had warned them that eating the fruit would bring death. Adam knew God's Word. When he disobeyed God, he said in effect, "God is a liar. I don't believe Him."

Fourth, God was Adam's friend, walking and talking with him in the garden. When Adam ate the fruit, he was saying, "I would rather have a piece of fruit instead of God. I love God's creation more than God. God is worthless."

Fifth, God was Adam's teacher and guide. But Adam took the fruit because he believed it would make him wise. His action shouted, "I don't want to listen to God's wisdom. I will have my own wisdom!"

So, you see, eating a little fruit in this case was a serious insult to God. In this one action Adam denied God's goodness, authority, truthfulness, worth, and wisdom. He utterly rejected God and broke covenant with Him. It was perfectly just and fair for God to punish Adam for this horrible sin.

12. Isn't it unfair that I'm a sinner because Adam and Eve sinned? Frankly, I think I would have done a better job.

First, we must never presume to judge God. Who are we to tell God that He is unfair? Our tiny minds cannot grasp His wisdom; our corrupt hearts cannot fathom His justice. Though we might want to question His justice, when we see His glory we will put our hands over our mouths and say with Job, "Therefore have I uttered that I understood not; things too wonderful for me, which I knew not" (Job 42:3).

Second, do you really think you could have done better than Adam? Consider the great advantages God gave the first man. He was made in the image of God, formed "very good" with flawless knowledge, righteousness, and holiness, and dominion over the creatures (Gen. 1:26, 31; Eph. 4:24; Col. 3:10). Adam's intelligence and moral purity were stunning. What better champion could the human race ask to represent them?

Furthermore, God put Adam in a perfect place, where all his needs and desires were met, and gave him a fulfilling job to do (Gen. 2). Adam walked and talked with God. And God did not require Adam to do some great, heroic thing, but only commanded him not to eat of one tree's fruit. Isn't it arrogant to think that we could have done better?

One day a man complained to his pastor that he would have done better than Adam. The pastor invited him over to his house. Then he said, "I need to leave for a while, so please make yourself at home. You can use and enjoy anything in my home. Just please do not open this small box on the table." After the minister left, the man walked around the house but kept coming back to the small box on the table. What was in it? He opened it just a bit. A mouse jumped out! When the minister returned home, he opened the box, and then said, "We don't really have to talk, do we, because now you know that you would not have done better than Adam."

Third, if it is unfair for Adam's sin to be counted against those who are one with him, then it is also unfair for Christ's righteousness to be counted to those who are one with Him. In other words, if we reject the Fall of Adam as the cause of our condemnation, then we have no basis to accept the obedience of Christ as the cause of our salvation.

But Paul accepts both and joins them together: "For as by one man's disobedience many were made sinners, so by the obedience of one shall many be made righteous" (Rom. 5:19). For the sake of the gospel, we must accept the fact that God can justly appoint one man to represent others within His covenants. Otherwise, we lose our hope that Christ can save us just as Adam lost us.

13. Why did God flood the earth?

Genesis 6:5-8 says, "God saw that the wickedness of man was great in the earth, and that every imagination of the thoughts of his heart was only evil continually. And it repented the Lord that he had made man on the earth, and it grieved him at his heart. And the Lord said, I will destroy man whom I have created from the face of the earth; both man, and beast, and the creeping thing, and the fowls of the air; for it repenteth me that I have made them. But Noah found grace in the eyes of the Lord."

God flooded the earth because of sin. Doesn't that tell us how bad sin is? The Scripture tells us that God saw into the hearts of mankind and saw that every thought was poisoned by evil all the time. That's how sinful we all are until God gives us a new heart. Sin deeply offends God. So the flood expressed God's righteous anger and judgment against sinners.

At the same time, it expressed His grace. God made a way of salvation: Noah's ark. God warns us that when Christ returns He will pour out His wrath on the earth, but with fire, not water. However, God has made a way of salvation: trusting in Jesus Christ. Christ is the ark of our safety because He obeyed God perfectly and died for sinners. Since He was plunged into the flood of God's wrath for sinners, He can save us from drowning in the lake of fire forever. So trust in Christ; hide in the Lord Jesus and the floods of God's wrath will never destroy you.

14. Is Lot's wife still there?

L ot and his family were living in the wicked city of Sodom when God came to destroy it (Gen. 19). God's angels brought Lot, his wife, and his daughters out of the city, warning them not to look back. But when God destroyed it with fire from the sky, Lot's wife looked back and she became a pillar of salt (Gen. 19:26). It was God's judgment upon her for loving this wicked world instead of fleeing to His salvation.

Sodom was in the region of the Jordan River (Gen. 13:10), and was probably located near the present Dead Sea. There are many salt pillars in the area even today. Could one of them be the remains of Lot's wife? Josephus, a Jewish man who lived in the time of the apostles of Christ, claimed to have seen the pillar of Lot's wife. We cannot know for sure. After thousands of years, if it was still there, we could not recognize it.

But we can learn a valuable lesson from Lot's wife, even if we cannot find her pillar. Jesus Christ said in Luke 17:28-31, "Likewise also as it was in the days of Lot; they did eat, they drank, they bought, they sold, they planted, they builded; but the same day that Lot went out of Sodom it rained fire and brimstone from heaven, and destroyed them all. Even thus shall it be in the day when the Son of man is revealed. In that day, he which shall be upon the housetop, and his stuff in the house, let him not come down to take it away: and he that is in the field, let him likewise not return back. Remember Lot's wife. Whosoever shall seek to save his life shall lose it; and whosoever shall lose his life shall preserve it."

When Christ comes on Judgment Day, people who love this world will be going about their business until they are suddenly swept away by God's wrath. We must not cling to our lives in this world. We must turn our back on sin. Only if we let go

29

of our earthly lives and follow Jesus will we be ready when He comes in glory.

Tough
Questions About
God

15. What does it mean that the ship Paul was on had the sign of Castor and Pollux?

When Paul was taken as a prisoner from the island of Malta to Italy, they sailed on a ship bearing the sign of the sons of the false god Zeus, the twins "Castor and Pollux" (Acts 28:11). They are also known as the Gemini, the Latin word for twins. Pagans believed that they were the patrons of sailors. The signs or images of these gods were probably put on the ship in hopes that they would keep it safe on its voyage, just as some people carry a rabbit's foot or charms for good luck today.

But imaginary gods and magic charms cannot protect us. Paul, when sailing on another ship, had just passed through a terrible storm that lasted for two weeks and wrecked the ship. Most likely the sailors were crying out to many gods and spirits. Not a single person of the 276 on board died, but not because of pagan gods or good luck charms. An angel had told Paul, "God hath given thee all them that sail with thee" (Acts 27:24).

It is the sovereign God who rules over the storms (Jonah 1). Psalm 107:25, 29 says, "He commandeth, and raiseth the stormy wind, which lifteth up the waves thereof ... He maketh the storm a calm, so that the waves thereof are still." Christ is King of the waves, and they must obey His voice (Matt. 14:32).

Does that mean that we can do foolish things and expect God to protect us? No, God works through means. Even after God promised to protect them, Paul told the soldiers on that ship that they would die unless they stopped the sailors from abandoning ship (Acts 17:30-31). We must work faithfully and wisely. But we do so knowing that it is God, not our works or any other power, that controls our lives.

Don't be like those foolish sailors who thought Castor and Pollux would help them in their troubles. Don't trust in idols, spirits, good luck charms, or magic trinkets to guide or protect you. Trust in the Lord, and be faithful to do your duty. As Joab once said, we must be brave and do what we can, and let the Lord do what seems good to Him (2 Sam. 10:12).

16. The Bible says that God's voice is in the thunder. What is He saying?

Psalm 29:3-4 says, "The voice of the LORD is upon the waters: the God of glory thundereth: the LORD is upon many waters. The voice of the LORD is powerful; the voice of the LORD is full of majesty." That doesn't mean that God is speaking words in the thunder. We find God's words to us in the Bible, for the Scriptures did not come from man's heart but from the Holy Spirit (2 Pet. 1:20-21).

But God does speak in thunder in another way. He speaks in thunder just as He speaks in everything else. When you got out of bed this morning, He spoke to you of His goodness in sparing your life through another night. When you sat down for breakfast this morning, He spoke to you of His fatherly care in providing you with food. When it thunders, He speaks to you of His power, greatness, and majesty. In this way, God's "voice" is in everything—in sickness and in health, in both happy and sad times. In fact, in this way God is speaking to us all the time and everywhere. It's too bad we don't realize this more often.

God speaks to us in nature about who He is (Rom. 1:19-20; Ps. 19:1-6), but we must come to know Him in a saving way in Jesus Christ. Faith comes by hearing the Word of God, and we need preachers to tell it to us (Rom. 10:14, 17). The thunder tells us that God is powerful and fearsome. But only the gospel of Christ tells us how to be saved from His wrath.

17. What does it mean to fear the Lord? Why does the Bible say God is terrible?

The Bible says that God is "terrible" in several places (Deut. 7:21; 10:17; Neh. 1:5; 4:14; 9:32; Ps. 47:2; 68:35, 76:12; 99:3; Jer. 20:11). This does not mean He is really bad, in the modern sense of terrible, but instead that He is fearsome and awe-inspiring. In other words, we should fear the Lord because of who He is.

What does it mean to fear the Lord? There are two different ways you can fear God. One is the fear of a slave. Imagine a soldier who is captured by the enemy, beaten, put in chains, and forced to labor as a slave. He hates his master. But he does his work to avoid punishment. I hope you don't treat your mom and dad this way. This is slavish fear (Rom. 8:15). It's the kind of fear that Satan and the demons have towards God (Mark 1:22-23; James 2:19).

But there is a better way to fear the Lord. It is to mix fear of His majesty with love for His glory and with hope in His mercy (Deut. 10:12; Ps. 33:18). It is to delight to fear God because you know Him as the great and fearsome God who faithfully keeps His covenant promises of love (Neh. 1:5, 11). This is childlike fear, for it has the deep respect and security a child has toward a good and loving father. You know he will discipline you, yet he will spare no cost to do you good (1 Pet. 1:14-19). You want to please God more than anything (2 Cor. 5:9-11). This is the kind of fear that God puts in His chosen people so that they will never turn away from Him (Jer. 32:40).

Let me give you an example. Your mother tells you to pick up your toys twice in one day, but you forget. Later your dad tells you, but you are busy with something else. Of course, you are doing wrong. But when your dad or mom become upset with you for not picking up your toys, you feel hurt and upset too. If you are upset only because you are afraid of a spanking, that is what we call slavish fear. Everybody who has an active conscience has that kind of fear for God. But if you are upset because you are sad you have displeased your mom and dad who love you so much, this is a deeper kind of fear which we call *childlike* fear. Childlike fear means that you treasure God's smile and avoid His frown more than all the smiles and frowns of this world.

Pray every day, "Lord, help me to have a childlike fear for Thee, for Thou art a great God who hates sin with a terrible hatred, but Thou also art a great God to help those who fear Thee in love."

18. Why did God make me left-handed? Am I weird?

Being left-handed is not weird at all. It's part of the way God made you, and it's no handicap. It's just part of your unique makeup, like having red hair or green eyes. Remember that you are God's servant and He made you for special purposes.

Even handicapped people are made by God (Exod. 4:11). We can trust His wisdom and love that He has good purposes for them. How much more then can we trust God to have a good purpose for making you left-handed.

Some very special people in history were left-handed. When God raised up a leader to save Israel from Moab, he sent Ehud, a left-handed man, to do the job. Ehud was very brave, killing the king of Moab in the king's own palace and then leading the army of Israel to victory (Judges 3:15-30).

The tribe of Benjamin had left-handed soldiers in their army that were so skilled they could sling a stone at a hair and not miss (Judg. 20:16). That's a good shot!

William Perkins, known as the "father of Puritanism," was born in England in 1558. He was crippled in his right hand so he had to write with his left hand. At first, he was a very bad boy. He got drunk and he toyed with witchcraft. But the Holy Spirit convinced him of his sin. He trusted in Christ. A godly man named Laurence Chaderton became his mentor at school. He found godly friends like Richard Greenham and Richard Rogers. They became like spiritual brothers to him.

Perkins became a great preacher. He could explain the deep things of the Bible in a way that ordinary people could understand. He helped criminals in prison to know Jesus Christ. He taught students at college. He became like a father to many other Christians.

He wrote many books, which contained thousands of pages. His books were translated into other languages like Dutch, German, Spanish, French, Italian, Irish, Welsh, Hungarian, and Czech, and read all over Europe and later in America. All those books were written with his left hand.

So don't worry about being left-handed. Trust God's goodness, and use your left hand for His glory. Who knows how He will use you in the future?

19. What are the seven spirits in Revelation 1:4b?

The Bible verse you are talking about is this: "… from him which is, and which was, and which is to come; and from the seven Spirits which are before his throne." Your question is not easy to answer. Some have regarded the "seven Spirits" to be angels, based on such texts as Revelation 15:1. But that seems unlikely, for Revelation 1:4 seems to put the "spirits" on the same level as the eternal God as the source of blessing.

Most likely, "seven Spirits" refers to the Holy Spirit as the Spirit of the exalted Christ who is poured out on the church with the fullness of covenantal blessings. As seven is the number of divine fullness, the sevenfold Spirit of Christ represents the fullness of God's grace.

The number seven reminds us of the many works the Spirit does, for He is the promised Spirit (Acts 2:33), the Spirit of truth (John 14:17), the Comforter who abides with His church (John 14:15, 18), the Spirit of life (Rom. 8:2), and the Spirit of resurrection (Rom. 8:11). Further, the Holy Spirit's fullness is evident as Regenerator, Enlightener, Teacher, Guide, Guest, Sanctifier, and Author of prayer. He convicts, draws, cleanses, assists, and seals God's elect.

Isaiah 11:2 gives seven titles to the Holy Spirit, "And [1] the spirit of the LORD shall rest upon him, the spirit of [2] wisdom and [3] understanding, the spirit of [4] counsel and [5] might, the spirit of [6] knowledge and of [7] the fear of the LORD." In context, this refers to God's gift of the Spirit to the great King descended from David, Jesus Christ.

Thus, Revelation 1:4-5 is the blessing of God the Father (who is, was, and is to come, v. 4a); God the Holy Spirit ("seven

Spirits," v. 4b); and God the Son (Jesus Christ, v. 5). That's why it's used as a salutation or benediction in church services, for it declares the fullness of the triune God as the source, the enabler, and the object of all true worship.

20. What does "omnipotent" mean?

Revelation 19:6 says, "And I heard as it were the voice of a great multitude, and as the voice of many waters, and as the voice of mighty thunderings, saying, Alleluia: for the Lord God omnipotent reigneth." Omnipotent comes from two Latin words: *omni*, which means "all," and *potens*, which means "powerful." So omnipotent means to be "all-powerful." The same idea is translated "almighty" in the Bible (Gen. 17:1; 28:3; Ps. 91:1; Rev. 1:8; 4:8).

Omnipotence is more than just having unlimited power, although that is true of God. "Is any thing too hard for the LORD?" (Gen. 18:14). Omnipotent means that God rules with supreme power over all. The Psalms say over and over again, "The LORD reigneth" (Ps. 93:1; 96:10; 97:1; 99:1). Yes, "the LORD shall reign for ever and ever" (Exod. 15:18). He will always be in control in every situation.

The great king Nebuchadnezzar was compelled to say, "I blessed the most High, and I praised and honoured him that liveth for ever, whose dominion is an everlasting dominion, and his kingdom is from generation to generation: and all the inhabitants of the earth are reputed as nothing: and he doeth according to his will in the army of heaven, and among the inhabitants of the earth: and none can stay his hand, or say unto him, What doest thou?" (Dan. 4:34-35).

Only God is omnipotent. Some people may be powerful. They may have important friends or big muscles or lots of money. Angels are even more powerful. We know that Satan is much more powerful than we are. But no one is all-powerful except God. All the mighty ones of heaven and earth cannot so much as lift a finger apart from the will of the Almighty.

I hope this is a wonderful comfort for you. It is comforting for God's people. Do you know why? Because it means that everything is in God's hand. Our own hearts, other people, sin and Satan can all be powerful enemies, but the Lord rules everything. Oh, what a precious truth that the Lord is always in control!

21. Luke 10:31 says that there came down a certain priest "by chance." Should we believe in chance?

From God's viewpoint nothing happens by chance. God has known and determined everything from all eternity (Isa. 46:10; Eph. 1:11). There really is no such thing as luck. Nothing is ultimately an accident or mere chance, if by that we mean it has no purpose. Everything has a purpose in God's good plan (Prov. 16:4, 9, 33; Rom. 8:28). Even the hairs of our head are numbered by God (Matt. 10:30).

From our limited viewpoint, however, sometimes we speak of things happening by chance or by accident. We mean that something is surprising or unplanned by us. If you come around a corner in school and bump into your teacher coming from the opposite direction, you might be very surprised and say, "It was just by chance (or accident) that we happened to meet."

There's really nothing wrong with saying this, providing you realize you are speaking from the way you see things and not from the way God sees things. However, it's not right to believe in good luck or bad luck, because the universe is not run by "luck" but the providence of a wise and good God. No fortune, fate, or charm controls your destiny, but God does.

God knows, plans, and sees everything. He is everywhere. Remember this when Satan tempts you to do bad things. But also, bring all your needs to God—also that math or spelling test you may have tomorrow or next week—for God can help you in everything. Come to Him with all your fears and needs, especially your soul's needs, remembering that nothing happens by chance with God.

22. God knows everything, so why did He create the devil? Why did God let the devil rebel against Him?

This is a difficult question. Whenever we ask "Why?" questions of God, we must make sure that we ask them in submission to His good and wise will, and not with a secret accusation that He has done wrong. "None can stay his hand, or say unto him, What doest thou?" (Dan. 4:35b). "Nay but, O man, who art thou that repliest against God? Shall the thing formed say to him that formed it, Why hast thou made me thus?" (Rom. 9:20).

There is a mystery surrounding God's eternal plan. But He did reveal that when He made His plan "before the foundation of the world," He did so for this purpose: "to the praise of the glory of his grace" (Eph. 1:4, 6). It is true that sin has brought immeasurable suffering to God's creation. Sin also brought immeasurable suffering to God's Son by God's plan, so God certainly did not permit sin lightly—He loves His Son. But although He hates sin, God decreed that angels and men would fall into sin because Christ's work of salvation would display God's glory in a far more spectacular and satisfying way to His elect angels and men.

God desired that we would know His wrath, power, and grace in the richest possible way. "What if God, willing to shew his wrath, and to make his power known, endured with much longsuffering the vessels of wrath fitted to destruction: and that he might make known the riches of his glory on the vessels of mercy, which he had afore prepared unto glory" (Rom. 9:22-23).

When we treasure God's glory above all things, then we can appreciate that this is good and right. But if we think man's glory is most important, then we will hate God for His decree. How sad that would be!

23. Can a person truly seek the Lord but be rejected by Him because that person is not chosen by God?

When someone asked Christ, "Are there few that be saved?" He said, "Strive to enter in at the strait gate: for many, I say unto you, will seek to enter in, and shall not be able" (Luke 13:24). The Lord Jesus urged us to strive, labor, and fight to enter into salvation. Faith and repentance are not easy. They are difficult and painful.

But He also warned that some will "seek" but "not be able." What does that mean? We always must read the Bible in context. In the next verses, Christ told a parable about people trying to get into a man's house after he locked the door. They claim to be his friends. But instead they are thrown out into a place of great sadness (Luke 13:28).

Why are these "seekers" thrown out? The master of the house says to them, "Depart from me, all ye workers of iniquity" (Luke 13:27). In other words, they wanted to be saved from hell, but not from sin. Christ warned, "Except ye repent, ye shall all likewise perish" (Luke 13:3).

There is no true seeking of God without repentance for sin. Isaiah 55:6-7 says, "Seek ye the LORD while he may be found, call ye upon him while he is near: let the wicked forsake his way, and the unrighteous man his thoughts: and let him return unto the LORD, and he will have mercy upon him; and to our God, for he will abundantly pardon." God is full of love and mercy. Everyone who truly seeks the Lord with faith and repentance will find Him (Deut. 4:29).

Nowhere, however, does the Bible say that someone could truly seek God in faith and repentance but God might reject him because he is not chosen by God. No one truly seeks God in vain. God said, "I said not unto the seed of Jacob, Seek ye me

45

in vain: I the LORD speak righteousness, I declare things that are right" (Isa. 45:19). God does not trick us.

It is inconceivable that someone could repent but not find grace with God, because repentance is God's gift through Christ (2 Tim. 2:25; Acts 5:31). Only those whom God has chosen will repent; no one can come to Christ unless the Father draws him (John 6:44).

Election is not an obstacle for faith; it's an encouragement to seek the Lord because without election no one would be saved. Here's a promise God revealed that's worth hanging onto: Christ said, "All that the Father giveth me shall come to me; and him that cometh to me I will in no wise cast out" (John 6:37). "In no wise cast out" means Jesus will never, ever reject anyone who truly comes to Him. How can He, when everyone who comes to Him does so because the Father gave them to Christ?

Tough
Questions About
Christ

24. How is Jesus God's only begotten Son if the Bible says angels and men are sons of God?

The Bible does call angels "the sons of God" (Job 1:6; 2:1). It also says that people who receive Christ and have the Holy Spirit are the sons or children of God (John 1:12; Rom. 8:14). However, it does call Jesus Christ God's "only begotten" Son (John 1:14, 18; 3:16, 18; 1 John 4:9). It also says, "For unto which of the angels said he at any time, Thou art my Son, this day have I begotten thee?" (Heb. 1:5).

This means that Christ is God's Son in a way that no angel or mere man could be. Men, women, and children become God's sons and daughters when God adopts them into His family (Eph. 1:5). They were not always God's children. In fact, unless they repent of their sins and turn to the Lord Jesus in faith, they will never be God's children (1 John 3:10).

Angels were the sons of God when God was creating the earth (Job 38:4-7). But they too were created by God. In fact, they were created by Christ (Col. 1:16). He already existed in the beginning (John 1:1). Therefore, the angels worship the Son (Heb. 1:6; Rev. 5:11-13). And so should we, because as the only begotten Son, He is God.

When the Heidelberg Catechism (Q. 33) asks, "Why is Christ called the only begotten Son of God, since we are also the children of God?", it answers, "Because Christ alone is the eternal and natural Son of God; but we are children adopted of God, by grace, for His sake."

When we say that Christ was "begotten" we are not saying that He had a beginning, for His goings forth are "from everlasting" (Micah 5:2). We call this Christ's eternal generation or eternal begetting. Christ is the natural Son of God because He shares in God's nature. He has the same glory as the Father (Heb. 1:3).

He has the same power and wisdom and love as the Father—all the fullness of God lives in the Son (Col. 2:9).

Isn't it amazing that God Himself would become a man and live among us?

25. Is "Christ" the last name of Jesus? Why does the Bible call Him "the Christ"?

I can understand why someone would think that the last name of Jesus Christ is "Christ." But sometimes the Bible calls Him "the Christ" (Matt. 16:16), or "Christ Jesus" (Rom. 8:1). That's because "Christ" is not His last name, but His title or office telling us of the work He came into the world to do.

The word "Christ" comes from the Greek word meaning "Anointed," just like "Messiah" is from the Hebrew word meaning "Anointed." In the Bible, when a person was chosen for a special job then people would anoint him, putting a little olive oil with sweet smelling fragrance on his head. They often used oil as we use lotion to make ourselves look and smell good (Ruth 3:3; Dan. 10:3; Matt. 6:17; see Esther 2:12).

There were three offices in Israel that were especially marked by anointing. They anointed priests to set them apart for their work of serving God in the tabernacle or temple (Exod. 28:41; 29:7). They anointed kings to show God had chosen them to rule over His people and defend them (1 Sam. 10:1). Prophets to whom God gave His Word also were anointed (1 Kings 19:16). The anointing with oil symbolized the gift of the Holy Spirit to help them to do these special works (1 Sam. 16:13; Isa. 61:1; Zech. 4:6, 14).

When the Bible calls Jesus "the Christ," it is saying that God has anointed Him far above anyone else (Heb. 1:9). Jesus has the Holy Spirit in super-abundance to share the Spirit with His people (John 1:33; 3:34). As the Christ, Jesus takes these three offices of prophet, priest, and king to a whole new level.

Christ is the ultimate prophet (Acts 3:22-23) who not only speaks God's Word but is God's Word to us (John 1:1). He is the great High Priest who offered Himself as a sacrifice for our sins and intercedes in heaven to save His people completely (Heb. 7:25; 10:11-12). He is the King of kings and Lord of lords who rules us by His Spirit and will one day come in His Father's glory (1 Tim. 6:14-15).

The title "Christ" is precious to believers. It promises us that there is a Prophet who can teach us the truth despite our ignorance and blindness. There is a Priest who can take away the guilt of our sins and bring us close to God. And there is a King who can conquer our sinful hearts and bring us into an eternal kingdom. As "Christians" we also bear this title because Christ makes us prophets who know and speak God's truth, priests who worship in God's presence and offer Him pleasing obedience, and kings who overcome Satan and rule over God's creation.

26. How did Jesus' death on the cross take away sins?

Sin brings God's curse. Galatians 3:10 says, "For as many as are of the works of the law are under the curse: for it is written, Cursed is every one that continueth not in all things which are written in the book of the law to do them." The law of God pronounces a curse against every sinner, condemning him to punishment. God's justice demands the punishment of all sin, for all sin is an attack on His honor.

As our substitute, Christ took the curse for us. Galatians 3:13 says, "Christ hath redeemed us from the curse of the law, being made a curse for us: for it is written, Cursed is every one that hangeth on a tree." Christ took away sins by taking on Himself the curse sinners deserved. This was publicly set forth in the way He died, hanging upon a wooden cross. (The word "tree" in the Bible can refer to a living tree or a piece of wood like a log or pole.)

Since Christ is the representative of His people, what He did satisfies God's law for everyone who trusts in Christ. Even though Christians still sin, God does not count it against them because Jesus paid the "ransom price" for their debt (Mark 10:45). How precious it is to trust in Christ as your perfect righteousness and to know that God no longer counts against you any of your sins! "Blessed is he whose transgression is forgiven, whose sin is covered. Blessed is the man unto whom the Lord imputeth not iniquity, and in whose spirit there is no guile" (Ps. 32:1-2). Christ took away sins by taking sin's punishment on Himself.

27. How come Jesus had to get baptized?

It really surprised John the Baptist when Jesus came to him to be baptized (Matt. 3:14). John was calling people to repent of sin. Their baptism in the Jordan River was a sign that they were confessing their sins, turning back to God, seeking His forgiveness, and fleeing from His wrath (Matt. 3:1-6; Luke 3:3, 7). John taught people that One was coming who was far greater than he was, and who would baptize them with the Holy Spirit (Matt. 3:11; Luke 3:16).

So you can understand John's shock when Christ came to him seeking baptism. Christ was not a sinner, but the holy Son of God (Luke 1:35). Should the Lord be baptized by one of His servants?

Why did Jesus get baptized? Jesus was baptized not for His sake but for the sake of His people. He came to identify with sinners and stand in their place before God (2 Cor. 5:21). He did it as God's servant "to fulfil all righteousness" (Matt. 3:15). Righteousness here means God's work to save sinners by making them right with Him through His fulfilling of the requirements of the law, including bearing the penalty for those who do not keep it.

Maybe Jesus had in mind a Scripture like Isaiah 42:6-7, where God promised Christ, "I the LORD have called thee *in righteousness,* and will hold thine hand, and will keep thee, and give thee for a covenant of the people, for a light of the Gentiles; to open the blind eyes, to bring out the prisoners from the prison, and them that sit in darkness out of the prison house."

Jesus' baptism is just one more way the Bible teaches that Jesus is a perfect and complete Savior for His people. It shows how He obeys the law and bears the punishment of sin for His people.

He was baptized with our baptism, and died our death, so that we could be raised with His resurrection. And only in this way can God not be angry with His people, who are all sinners in themselves. No wonder God responded to Jesus' baptism by saying, "This is my beloved Son, in whom I am well pleased" (Matt. 3:17; see Isa. 42:1).

Oh, I hope that you too may feel your need and find such a rich Savior for such poor sinners as we are! Bring all your sins to God and ask God to wash you clean, to baptize you with His Spirit in the name of the Lord Jesus Christ who was baptized for all His people.

28. What did Christ mean when He said He came to bring a sword? Doesn't He love peace?

Jesus said in Matthew 10:34b-36, "I came not to send peace, but a sword. For I am come to set a man at variance against his father, and the daughter against her mother, and the daughter in law against her mother in law. And a man's foes shall be they of his own household."

Jesus loves peace. He is the Prince of peace who builds up a kingdom of peace (Isa. 9:6-7). He calls men to be merciful, forgiving peacemakers (Matt. 5:7, 8). But Christ knew that His teaching would not bring peace to all men. Those whom the Father gave to Christ would receive His Word, believe it, and obey it (John 17:6). But the world hates Christ because His Word shows them their sins (John 3:19-20). As a result, the world will also hate those who follow Christ (John 15:18). The people of the world will persecute them, for Christ's sake (Matt. 5:10-12).

When Christ said He came to bring a sword, he was not talking about a weapon that kills. He was talking about the truth that divides men into two groups: believers and unbelievers. Even in the same family, some may believe and others not. When that happens, the believers can no longer join with the others in sinning, and unbelievers think that believers are strange and may say hard things to them (1 Pet. 4:4).

You must make a choice. It is good to obey your parents. It is good to be friends with your family. But when they go against God will you follow them? Or will you follow Jesus Christ?

Jesus gave this sobering warning, "Whosoever therefore shall confess me before men, him will I confess also before my Father which is in heaven. But whosoever shall deny me before men, him will I also deny before my Father which is in heaven" (Matt. 10:32-33).

29. Why did Jesus have to suffer so much?

Jesus suffered horribly on the cross. It was so bad that even before He was crucified just the thought of it made Him fall down on the ground, cry out to God in prayer, and sweat drops of blood wrung from Him by terrible stress (Mark 14:34-36; Luke 22:44). Dying on a cross was so painful and disgusting that people did not even like to talk about crucifixion (I Cor. 1:23). Jesus died as one who had been forsaken of God and had experienced spiritual darkness far worse than the physical darkness around Him that day (Matt. 27:45-46).

Why did it have to be so hard? Certainly it was not because of Christ. God loved His Son with a love beyond anything the angels can understand. He was totally pleased with Him and told Him so repeatedly (Luke 3:22; 9:35).

But God hates sin with a holy anger, wrath, and righteous outrage (Rom. 1:18; 2:5, 8-9). God is slow to anger, patient and self-controlled, but sin makes Him as furious and fierce as a fire that burns up oceans and melts mountains (Nahum 1:2-6). Christ died for our sins (I Cor. 15:3). He is the propitiation for our sins (Rom. 3:25), which means that all the fury of God's offended justice was poured out on Him instead of us.

Christ died as a substitute. Let me try to explain that with a story. One day a boy (let's call him Tom) was naughty in school. So the teacher told Tom that he'll have to stand in the corner for ten minutes. The teacher, who was new in the class, did not know that Tom could not stand that long because he was handicapped in his legs.

But there was another boy (let's call him Henry) in the class who raised his hand, and asked: "Teacher, may I stand in the corner for Tom?"

The teacher looked surprised: "But why, Henry, would you want to stand in the corner for Tom?" she asked. "You didn't do anything bad!"

"Well," Henry said, a bit shyly, "Tom is my friend, and I know that Tom can't stand that long all by himself." So the teacher let Henry stand in the corner. Tom was so grateful to Henry!

Then the teacher said, "Boys and girls, I want you to learn from what you have just seen. Henry took the place of Tom because Tom can't bear his punishment. Henry was his substitute. The Lord Jesus Christ took the place of lost sinners because they can't pay for the punishment of their sins. Just because God loves them, Jesus became their substitute. But children, Jesus didn't just stand in the corner. Our sins deserved terrible suffering in hell. How wonderful it is that Jesus was willing to suffer God's anger against sin as our substitute!"

30. How can Jesus be sitting at God's right hand? Isn't He everywhere? Isn't He with us?

The Lord Jesus is indeed with His people. He said, "I am with you alway, even unto the end of the world" (Matt. 28:20). He promised to be present especially when His church gathers together in His name (Matt. 18:20). The Bible also says that God's Son is upholding all the universe by the word of His power (Heb. 1:3), so He is everywhere, even to the farthest star.

However, the Bible also says that after Christ rose from the dead, forty days later He went up into heaven and sat down at God's right hand (Acts 1:3; Ps. 110:1; Rom. 8:34). The apostles, who spoke with Him after He rose from the dead, watched Jesus go up into the sky until a cloud hid Him from sight (Acts 1:9). Stephen even saw the Lord Jesus standing at God's right hand shortly before Stephen was killed by an angry mob because of his bold preaching (Acts 7:55).

How can He be there and here and everywhere? When we talk about Jesus being in a place, we can understand Him being present in three ways: as a man, as the giver of the Holy Spirit, and as God the Son.

As a man, Christ is at the right hand of God in heaven. Jesus is still truly human. His human body can only be in one place at a time. He went up to heaven. He will remain there until He comes back on Judgment Day. What a joy it is to know that God has honored our human nature far above all the angels! For in lifting up Christ, God guaranteed that He will lift up to heaven everyone who belongs to Christ (Eph. 2:6-7).

As the giver of the Holy Spirit, Christ lives inside of every Christian's heart by the Spirit. Christ has received the Holy Spirit in overflowing measure. He poured out that same Spirit upon His people at Pentecost (Acts 2:32-33). Now we are one with Him by the Spirit, and He is always with us. What a comfort this is, for our King is always there to give us power and wisdom to serve Him and to build His church (Matt. 28:18-20).

As God the Son, Christ has always been present in all places. Just like the Father, the Son is omnipresent. He is the One who holds the universe together (Col. 1:17). Even before the gospel is preached in a place, the Son of God is there, preparing the people and the place for the coming of His kingdom. When we hear about big things happening in faraway nations, or the motions of planets, meteors, and comets, we can rest assured that Jesus is there and He is Lord.

31. Did Jesus have a wife?

Jesus is a real man, in all ways like us except without sin (Heb. 2:14; 4:15). He had a mother, Mary, brothers, sisters, and friends like Simon Peter, James, John, Mary Magdalene, Joanna, and Susanna (Matt. 10:2-3; Luke 8:2-3). He honored marriage and loved children (Matt. 19:4-6, 14-15). But He never got married or had any children of His own.

Why? For one thing, Jesus Christ is both God and man (John 1:1, 14). It would not have been right for a particular woman to be married to God. Furthermore, Christ has a special mission in life that would have made it very hard for Him to marry and have a family. He never owned a home (Luke 9:58). After three busy years of preaching, teaching, healing, and training leaders, Christ died for sinners on the cross, rose from the dead, and went up into heaven.

Another reason that He did not marry a wife is that Christ has a spiritual bride. It's not just one person, but all the people God gave to His Son to save. The Bible calls Jesus the "bridegroom" of His people (Mark 2:19-20; John 3:29). He loved them so much that He gave Himself for them to save them from sin and make them perfectly beautiful (Eph. 5:25-27).

Right now God's Spirit, through the preaching of the Word, helps get us ready to meet our heavenly Husband in all purity (2 Cor. 11:2). One day Christ will come back for His church. They will celebrate their wedding feast with the Lord, dressed in the spiritual loveliness that He gave them (Matt. 22:1-14; Rev. 19:7-9). Then Christ and His bride will live together forever.

Christ's redemption of His people is the greatest love story ever told. Earthly marriage is just a faint picture of the amazing love He has for every Christian. If you are a Christian, then pray for God to fill you with the knowledge of how much Christ loves you (Eph. 3:19). If not, then pray for God the Father to wed your heart to Jesus Christ forever.

Tough Questions About Salvation

32. How does the Lord tell you if you get a new heart?

The gift of a new heart is part of God's work of saving a sinner. It produces conversion, or the turning of a sinner back to God in humility and obedience. Ezekiel 36:26-27 says, "A new heart also will I give you, and a new spirit will I put within you: and I will take away the stony heart out of your flesh, and I will give you an heart of flesh. And I will put my spirit within you, and cause you to walk in my statutes, and ye shall keep my judgments, and do them."

The Lord doesn't speak to us directly from heaven to tell us that we have received a new heart. Rather, the Bible tells us that we may know that we have a new heart by the "fruits" of it in our lives (Matt. 7:16; Gal. 5:22). This means that a new heart shows itself in how we think, speak, and act.

We can know that we know God if we walk in the light of God's Word, confess our sin, trust in Christ as our sacrifice and Advocate to gain us acceptance with God, and walk in obedience to God's commands, especially by loving each other and separating ourselves from the evil ways of this world (1 John 1–2). Becoming a Christian doesn't mean that you don't sin anymore but it does mean that God's Word now rules your heart and conduct instead of sin. "But God be thanked, that ye were the servants of sin, but ye have obeyed from the heart that form of doctrine which was delivered you" (Rom. 6:17).

When God saves you, it produces many fruits. Here are some of them: love for God and all the things of God, such as the Bible, the church, and prayer; hatred for all that God hates, such as sin, Satan, and placing anything above God; sadness for all the sins we commit when we don't love God and love people as we should; a sense of our need to be saved from all our sins by God through His Son; a humble and thankful heart toward God for the salvation He has provided; the desire to thankfully obey God's law at all times, even though we often fail.

The Lord loves to convert boys and girls. In fact, He often gives new hearts to people when they are young. So now is the best time for you to ask Him to give you a new heart and love for Him. Don't be afraid to pray to God for a new heart. He loves to hear the prayers of young children. Try to pray this prayer: "Lord, show me who I am. Show me who Thou art. Please give me a new heart, and help me to repent and to believe in Jesus Christ alone for salvation."

33. How could the demoniac's father have unbelief if he believed?

God's people experience the same thing today. They have faith, and some have great faith (Matt. 8:10; 15:28), but sadly too many of them have only a little faith (Matt. 6:30). As a result life's circumstances quickly cast them into fear (Matt. 8:26; 14:31). Their little faith is like a dim light so that it's hard for them to see God's Word (Matt. 16:8-12). Where there is little faith, there remains much unbelief.

But this man was not ruled by unbelief. He had true, saving faith. Look how his faith made his heart tender and broken. He cried out "with tears" (Mark 9:24). When free grace enters your life you become soft before God: your heart melts; you become pliable and teachable. Has that happened to you? Have you laid your weapons down? Is your heart made tender before God?

He was not satisfied with a weak faith. He had a troubling sense of his remaining unbelief, and wanted to conquer it. That sent him crying to the Savior, "Help thou my unbelief." Do you have that? Do you hate your unbelief? Do you war against it? You see, if you're a true believer you're involved in spiritual warfare; you are fighting a holy war indeed.

This father wanted more than a solution to his earthly problems; he hungered and thirsted for more faith. If you know Jesus Christ, you want to know Him better. You come to church with the hope in your heart to meet God. You pray because you desire to meet God and grow. You open the Bible in hope that God will meet you in the pages of His Word. Your heart's cry is, "I want to love Him more. I want to worship Him more. I want to see more of who He is. I want to enjoy Him more. I want to please Him more." The disciples said to the Lord, "Increase our faith" (Luke 17:5). If you can't say that is your soul's desire, then you are not a Christian.

If you do pant after God, then do not let your remaining unbelief discourage you. Have you ever played tug-of-war with a rope and a group of people on each end? Each group tries to pull the rope their way to see who is strongest. Well, faith and unbelief are like that in a Christian. Faith pulls one way and unbelief, the other. Happily, by the Holy Spirit's grace, faith will ultimately win the war, though it may lose some skirmishes along the way.

Don't look down on this man. Join him. Make his prayer your own, saying, "Lord, I believe; help thou mine unbelief."

34. What's the difference between the Pharisee and the publican in Jesus' parable?

Christ told this story to warn people who trusted in themselves that they were self-righteous and looked down on other people: "Two men went up into the temple to pray; the one a Pharisee, and the other a publican. The Pharisee stood and prayed thus with himself, God, I thank thee, that I am not as other men are, extortioners, unjust, adulterers, or even as this publican. I fast twice in the week, I give tithes of all that I possess."

Jesus continued, "And the publican, standing afar off, would not lift up so much as his eyes unto heaven, but smote upon his breast, saying, God be merciful to me a sinner. I tell you, this man went down to his house justified rather than the other: for every one that exalteth himself shall be abased; and he that humbleth himself shall be exalted" (Luke 18:10-14).

What's the difference? The Pharisee went into God's presence without fear and trembling; the publican stood far off full of fear and trembling. He did not feel worthy to pray to God, not even raising his eyes. The Pharisee had an arrogant heart, but the publican struck himself on the chest to show his broken heart.

The Pharisee had no sense of urgency or need, making more of an announcement than a prayer. The publican was gripped with his urgent need, crying out for mercy. The Pharisee counted his good deeds; the publican confessed his sinfulness and need. The Pharisee only paid attention to outward actions; the publican paid attention to the problem of his nature as a sinner. The Pharisee compared himself to other men; the publican compared himself to God.

The Pharisee asked for nothing, confessed nothing, and went home with nothing. He justified himself, but remained a condemned sinner before God. The publican asked for everything, confessed everything, and went home with everything. Regardless of what men might think of him, he was a saved sinner, justified by the grace of God.

Which are you, the Pharisee or the publican? Perhaps you feel like you are both; if so, pray that God will help you purge out "the Pharisee" that is within you, so that you, like the publican, may base all your hopes for salvation on God's mercy alone.

35. What is justification? How can God justify sinners if He is just and righteous?

The bedrock of true religion is the belief that the Judge of all the earth will do right (Gen. 18:25). The foundation of our faith is the belief that this Judge will justify sinners if they trust in Christ alone for salvation (Gal. 2:16). If this is not true, then Christ died for nothing (Gal. 2:21).

Martin Luther said that justification by faith alone is the truth by which the church stands or falls. John Calvin said justification is the main hinge on which religion turns. What is justification by faith alone?

When a person is brought into a courtroom and charged with a crime, the judge has two options. He may condemn him as guilty of breaking the law and sentence him to be punished. Or he may justify him, declaring him to be righteous in the sight of the law, and release him from all charges.

The amazing promise of the Bible is that God the Judge will justify ungodly sinners who trust in Jesus Christ alone (Rom. 4:5). He does not justify them based upon their own good works (Gal. 2:16). He does not bend His law and say they are guilty but He'll let them go because He has a soft heart. Rather, He looks for a ground on which to account them righteous (Gen. 15:6). This ground is the perfect righteousness and atoning sacrifice of Christ.

All their sins are forgiven and all the punishment due to them is gone (Ps. 32:1-2; 103:12). His anger against them for their sins is pacified and He promises never to burn in wrath against them again (Isa. 54:9-10).

How can God do that? He does that because He has joined the believer to Jesus Christ, and Christ is our righteousness (1 Cor. 1:30). Christ obeyed God, and His perfect righteousness is counted to all who are in Him (Rom. 5:19). Christ suffered the punishment God's justice demands for sin, so that God can justify sinners and still be a just Judge (Rom. 3:25-26).

What a gift! Have you received Christ as your only righteousness?

36. What happens if I am a Christian, do loads of bad stuff, but don't repent before I die?

This question could come from different angles. On the one hand, it might come from a person who claims to be a Christian but has not repented of sin. He has a kind of belief in God, but does not grieve over sin nor turn from it to God. To such a person, Christ says in Mark 1:15, "The time is fulfilled, and the kingdom of God is at hand: repent ye, and believe the gospel."

He warns in Luke 13:3, "Except ye repent, ye shall all likewise perish." There is no salvation without repentance over our sins. If this is you, then fear, turn from evil, and cry out for the gift of wholehearted repentance!

On the other hand, this question might come from a person who does repent, but is anxious because much sin still remains in his life. He does hate sin. He does love God. He fights against sin and often obeys God, although imperfectly. But sometimes the burden of his remaining sins overwhelms him with sadness.

The plain truth is, sin will be a problem for the Christian as long as he lives. We shall all do loads of bad stuff before we die. The false Christian is not troubled by his sins. The true Christian learns more and more to hate his sins and to flee from them. But our salvation does not depend on what we do or don't do; it rests wholly on the work of Christ.

To such a person Christ says in Matthew 5:3-4, "Blessed are the poor in spirit: for theirs is the kingdom of heaven. Blessed are they that mourn: for they shall be comforted." When you tremble at God's Word and feel spiritually poor, you are in the best position to receive grace. If this is you, be encouraged! Christ is full of mercy to the poor in spirit.

37. How can someone go to church on Sunday but act like the world for the rest of the week?

Quite easily. Our hearts are naturally prone to such hypocrisy. We can go to church for a number of reasons, including custom, pleasing parents or grandparents, seeing our friends, quieting a guilty conscience, or enjoying learning or music. But none of those requires a heart that is changed by the gospel.

The Lord said through Isaiah, "This people draw near me with their mouth, and with their lips do honour me, but have removed their heart far from me" (Isa. 29:13). Jesus said the same about His generation over 700 years later (Matt. 15:8). It's still true.

Christ warned us that just because we hear the preaching of the Word that does not make us a Christian. He told the parable of the soils to explain that most people who listen to the Word do not really benefit from it (Luke 8:4-15). Some people are not affected by the Word at all, like water running off a rock. Others have a superficial, emotional response, but their hearts remain hard and the Word has no roots in them.

Still other people try to embrace the Word while hanging on to the love of this world. Without cutting the roots of worldliness by repentance, ultimately God's truth gets choked out by earthly concerns. It's not getting people into church that saves them, but getting the Word into their hearts.

The Lord therefore said, "Take heed therefore how ye hear" (Luke 8:18). Instead of being distracted by hypocrites, make sure you're not a hypocrite. Pray that God would save you. Listen, think, believe, feel, and obey the Word. God is worthy to be served, loved, and feared with all our hearts and all our souls.

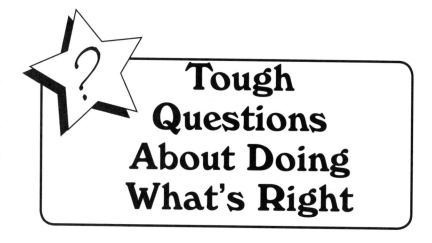

Tough Questions About Doing What's Right

38. The Bible says to turn the other cheek and to give an eye for an eye and a tooth for a tooth. Which should we believe?

We should believe and obey both. We find both principles in the same Bible, even in the same book of the Bible. In Romans 12:14 it says, "Bless them which persecute you: bless, and curse not." However in Romans 13:4 we read of the civil government, "But if thou do that which is evil, be afraid; for he beareth not the sword in vain: for he is the minister of God, a revenger to execute wrath upon him that doeth evil." Therefore, our personal lives should be characterized by love and forgiveness for our enemies, but the government has a responsibility to use force to restrain and punish criminals.

In the court of justice, society must be ruled by the principle of "eye for eye, tooth for tooth" (Exod. 21:24; Lev. 24:20; Deut. 19:21). This does not mean that criminals should be cut up, but that crimes should be punished with fair penalties (Exod. 21:26-27). For the good order of society, justice must be maintained. Criminals must be punished for their crimes.

In our private lives, however, we are to "turn the other cheek" when other people abuse us. We are not to return evil for evil, but love for evil. Sometimes this is very hard, but when we see the love of Jesus for the kinds of sinners we are, there are times in our lives when we may find this easy to do.

39. What does "turn the other cheek" mean? Is self-defense against your religion?

That depends what you mean by self-defense. If you mean physically attacked, the answer is no, self-defense is not against the Christian faith. If you mean being charged with a crime or sued in a court of law, the answer is also no when the truth is at stake. If you mean being personally challenged or criticized, in some cases self-defense is called for when the glory of God is at stake, and in other cases we are wisest to give our opponent no answer.

What did the Lord mean then by "turn the other cheek"? He said in Matthew 5:39, "Whosoever shall smite thee on thy right cheek, turn to him the other also." The picture here is of someone slapping you across the face in a public insult (2 Cor. 11:20). Your face stings, your pride is injured, and your anger flares. Christ called us to renounce personal vengeance however, swallow our pride, and love our enemy.

On the one hand, we note that our Lord was not describing a stab with a sword but a slap in the face. Therefore He did not prohibit self-defense when someone threatens us with physical harm. God's prohibition of murder implies that human life, including your life, is precious and should be protected from wrongful harm. It is good and right to care for and protect our bodies so long as it does not distract us from the path of duty (Eph. 5:28-29).

On the other hand, we must willingly part with our honor before men when criticized and insulted. Most of the time we are ready to defend ourselves too quickly. We must learn the wisdom of Jesus who often did not answer His accusers (Isa. 53:7; Matt. 26:63; 27:12, 14). We must pray for guidance in such cases. If we do feel that the truth needs to be spoken, we must do so in love, not answering our attacker in the same bitter spirit with which he confronts us.

Above all, however, we must be concerned to seek grace to defend the name of God more than our own name. For this, we need the continual influence of the Holy Spirit in our lives.

The next time someone says something bad about you or hurts you, try to think about how many times people said bad things about Jesus and how he kept loving sinners. Pray to the Lord that you may love your brother, sister, or friend when he hurts you. Say to Him, "Lord, give me a new heart, and make me like Jesus, so that I will show love for hatred, and be nice to people when they are mean to me."

40. What's wrong with playing the lottery?

Lottery fever is running rampant yet again. This year three lottery winners received lump sums of about $100 million each. Our society has succumbed to "lotto lust." Regularly our mailbox contains promises of prizes, sweepstakes, winning numbers, bonuses, or questions like, "What would you do with $1,000,000?"

What's wrong with the lottery? Money is not evil. A lot of good can be done with money, and God encourages us to work hard and earn money so that we can share it with those in need (Eph. 4:28). The rich can enjoy their wealth and be rich in good works (1 Tim. 6:17-18).

But playing the lottery springs from an evil and destructive motive. There is no reason to gamble except out of a desire to get rich. In 1 Timothy 6:9-10 it says, "But they that will be rich fall into temptation and a snare, and into many foolish and hurtful lusts, which drown men in destruction and perdition. For the love of money is the root of all evil: which while some coveted after, they have erred from the faith, and pierced themselves through with many sorrows." God has commanded us, "Thou shalt not covet" (Exod. 20:17), and playing the lottery caters to coveting just as surely as viewing pornography caters to illicit sexual lust.

The lottery promotes proud delusions of being God instead of faithful stewardship of what we have. Whether we win the jackpot or simply fantasize about what we would do with it, the desire to win millions is essentially the same as man's first sin in Paradise: "ye shall be as gods" (Gen. 3:5). We waste our time and money when the chances of winning the lottery are not one-in-a-million, but closer to one in a hundred million—or worse.

Sadly, many lottery players are poor, and playing the lottery makes more than 99 percent of them even poorer.

Last, winning the lottery distorts your relationships. The Bible warns, "The rich hath many friends" (Prov. 14:20)—false friends who want their money. Wealth isolates you. It thrusts you into a position of responsibility for which you are not prepared: managing massive resources. Worst of all, it makes it very difficult for you to escape hell and enter God's kingdom (Matt. 19:24). When money abounds, people often forget God (Deut. 8:11-18).

Far better to pray for God to provide your needs but not make you rich, lest you say, "Who is the Lord?" (Prov. 30:7-9). Godliness with contentment is true riches (1 Tim. 6:6).

41. Is it murder to kill a deer? What if you hit it with your car?

We need to realize that there is no sin in accidentally killing anything, whether an animal or a human being. If a deer runs out in front of your car and is killed by the impact, there is not much you can do about it. Similarly if a man is cutting wood with an ax and without warning the axhead flies off and kills another man, God's law protects the first man from being punished (Deut. 19:5). However, if someone knows that something is dangerous and neglects safety, then he is accountable when someone gets killed (Exod. 21:28-29).

In God's original creation there was no death or killing. People and animals ate plants and not meat (Gen. 1:29-30). But with sin, death entered the world (Gen. 2:17; Rom. 5:12). God then gave His approval to killing animals for clothing (Gen. 3:21) and for sacrifices in worship (Gen. 4:4). After the flood, God gave Noah permission to kill animals for food (Gen. 9:3). But the Lord said that we must never murder human beings because they were created in God's image. In fact, he said that murderers should be put to death (Gen. 9:5-6).

Therefore it is not murder to kill a plant or animal. We have the right to harvest and use plants for our benefit. We also have the God-given liberty to kill animals and use their skins, meat, and other body parts. Animals are not people.

But as stewards of God's creation we do not have the right to destroy plants and animals for no good reason (Deut. 20:19). God's law puts some limits on killing animals, telling us to leave some alive (Lev. 22:28; Deut. 22:6-7). We also should not hunt animals just for the thrill of the kill. It's never good to enjoy death. Animals and plants are God's good creations, and we should use them to His glory.

42. What does Jesus mean by saying we must hate our parents, brothers, and sisters?

In Luke 14:26, Christ said, "If any man come to me, and hate not his father, and mother, and wife, and children, and brethren, and sisters, yea, and his own life also, he cannot be my disciple." These are strong words. What did our Lord mean?

Jesus said that He did not come to abolish the law but to fulfill it (Matt. 5:17). So His teachings must fit with God's commandments to honor our father and our mother (Exod. 20:12) and to love our neighbor, including our brothers and sisters, as ourselves (Lev. 19:18).

When Jesus said we must "hate" our families and our own lives to be His disciples, He was saying that we must love Him far above all of them. God must have our whole heart (Mark 12:30). He said in another Scripture, "He that loveth father or mother more than me is not worthy of me: and he that loveth son or daughter more than me is not worthy of me" (Matt. 10:37).

Sometimes obeying the Lord will make a parent, brother, or friend mad at you. Christ's teachings will divide families when one person follows Christ but others do not (Matt. 10:34-35). If that happens to you, then you must still confess Christ before men (Matt. 10:32-33).

Having a parent or brother or sister against you might hurt you deeply. But Jesus said that we must take up our crosses and follow Him. It's costly to be a Christian (Luke 14:27-28). So we keep on loving our families and praying for them. But Christ is our Lord.

43. What do I do for people who constantly misuse God's name?

This is a problem. God loves His name and expects us to treat it with reverence. He says in the Third Commandment, "Thou shalt not take the name of the LORD thy God in vain; for the LORD will not hold him guiltless that taketh his name in vain" (Exod. 20:7). "In vain" means treating God's name as if it were nothing, unimportant, without significance.

We should speak of God with a sense that He is the most important Being. If we could put God on one side of a scale and all the universe on the other, then they would be lighter than a feather compared to the weight of His glory (Isa. 40:15). God is determined to glorify His name in all the world (Mal. 1:11).

But nothing is more common today than for people to use "God," "Lord," "Jesus," or "Christ" as meaningless words or even curses. What can we do?

First, examine yourself. Is your own speech clean and reverent? Do you regard God with reverence? Do you honor Him with your actions?

Second, pray for your friend. Christ taught us to pray, "Our Father which art in heaven, hallowed be thy name." We are asking that people would treat God's name as sacred and holy. Ask God for wisdom and boldness to speak for Him.

Third, speak with your friend privately. Show him respect.

Fourth, tell him your concern with humility and gentleness. Emphasize the greatness and goodness of God: He is worthy to have His name honored.

Fifth, do not nag. Instead be patient and keep praying. J. C. Ryle, a great Christian preacher, was converted after a friend rebuked him for taking the Lord's name in vain. Who knows what God might do for your friend?

44. I'm always reading about brave men and heroes. Can women be brave too?

Yes, of course. Many women have been brave for the Lord. Ruth left her home and family out of love for her mother-in-law and faith in the God of Israel (Ruth 1:16; 2:12). Think of how brave and wise Abigail was, going out to stop David and his army from killing her foolish husband (1 Sam. 25). Or who can forget the bravery of Queen Esther (Esther 4:16), risking her life to protect her people, the Jews, from being destroyed by wicked Haman?

Queen Marguerite of Navarre was also brave. Navarre was a kingdom on the northern border between modern Spain and France. She was born in France in 1492. She trusted in Christ alone through the preaching of Jacques Lefevre D'Etaples.

Marguerite's brother, Francis, became the king of France. She tried to bring the Reformation to France, but this was dangerous. When her friend, the Count of Hohenlohe, tried to publish *The Book of the Cross* in France, the king stopped him and made it against the law to publish any books of Reformed Christianity. However, the love of King Francis I for his sister protected her from the plots of many who would do her harm.

Even though Marguerite could not stop the persecution of Reformed Christians in France, she did what she could to protect them. She was not ashamed to stand with those imprisoned for their faith in Christ. Once her husband, the king of Navarre, shouted at her and struck her across the face for her worship of the Lord. But she persevered in the faith. Her daughter, Jeanne d'Albret, carried on her legacy of faithfulness in the midst of terrible wars.

Never think that only men are brave Christians. Many godly women have stood firm in the strength of the Lord, and they are examples to us all.

45. How can I be a good witness in school? I'm scared that everyone will laugh at me and call me a religious fanatic.

Allow me to give you three hints.

First, remember that the best source of strength for public witnessing before others is your *private praying* with God. Paul wrote in Ephesians 6:10, "Finally, my brethren, be strong in the Lord, and in the power of his might." Later he said we must be praying all the time (v. 18) and even asked his friends to pray for his own courage to speak for Christ (v. 19).

If you walk close to God in private, you will not stray too far from His ways in public. The closer you feel to God the more His smiles and frowns will determine your actions rather than the smiles and frowns of your peers. This is what we call the fear of God: the childlike desire to please our Father above all. Seek grace to cultivate it.

Second, remember that your *heart's attitude* is critical for being a good witness both in your conversation and in your walk. Peter wrote in 1 Peter 3:15-16, "But sanctify the Lord God in your hearts: and be ready always to give an answer to every man that asketh you a reason of the hope that is in you with meekness and fear: having a good conscience; that, whereas they speak evil of you, as of evildoers, they may be ashamed that falsely accuse your good conversation in Christ."

Allow your walk to set a corrective example, but don't carry yourself with an over-righteous attitude. Avoid superiority like a plague. When your example appears insufficient, then you must correct another person verbally, as I discussed earlier (Q. 43).

Third, remember that your peers *respect you for doing God's will* much more than you realize. Deep in your heart, don't you respect that person most who dares to live right when he has a humble and reverent attitude? And you don't always tell that person, do you? Well, your peers will feel the same way about you. Their respect for you will come out in little ways. In a group they may even laugh at you, but in private they may very well come to you first for advice.

People, young or old, are too afraid of what their peers think of them. *Be true to God above all, be yourself as much as possible, and don't waste excessive time worrying about what your peers think.* Be kind, friendly, and loving and you will never run short of friends. Above all, be most concerned about what God thinks of you. That has lasting value. Your peer's attitudes can change daily. Besides, to whom must you give an eternal account on the great Judgment Day—to God or to your peers?

46. What does Psalm 1 mean by "he that walketh not in the counsel of the ungodly"?

Psalm 1:1-2 says, "Blessed is the man that walketh not in the counsel of the ungodly, nor standeth in the way of sinners, nor sitteth in the seat of the scornful. But his delight is in the law of the Lord; and in his law doth he meditate day and night."

This is the very beginning of the Psalms and is very important. It tells us the kind of person that God smiles upon and gives everlasting happiness to, even if right now that person is going through troubles. "Walk" means how you live your life. "Counsel" means the wisdom that guides your decisions and shapes your plans. So it's saying that if we want God's blessing on our lives, then we must not follow the ideas and beliefs of those who do not love God.

People who work with computers use the expression, "Garbage In, Garbage Out" (GIGO). Nutrition experts tell us you are what you eat. The same is true spiritually. What you choose to fill your mind will rule your life. If you read bad books, watch worldly TV shows, study under wicked teachers, look at inappropriate images and videos online, spend most of your time with sinful friends, and listen to corrupt music, then how can you expect not to follow the world in its sinful ways? Do you think that going to church a couple of hours a week will make up for the 100+ hours soaking up the counsel of the wicked?

What is the alternative? We must meditate on the Word of God. Meditation is not emptying your mind of all thought by repeating special words. Christian meditation is filling your mind with thoughts and feelings about what God says in the Bible.

Meditation is not complicated. It's like taking a piece of candy into your mouth and sucking on it till you get as much sweetness out as you can. You take something you read in the

Bible or heard in a sermon. You think about what it means. You compare it to other things you know. You preach it to yourself. You talk to God about it in prayer. You use it to stir up your feelings. You make decisions based on what it says.

But how can you delight in the Word of God if you don't like it and find it boring? You need God to put new desires in your heart. Ask the Lord to show you that you need to be born again to love the Lord and be truly happy. Ask the Lord to keep you from sinful things, sinful thoughts, sinful places, and sinful people. Ask Him to save you! And then ask Him to help you to grow more and more into a Psalm 1 person who delights in His Word all the time.

Tough Questions About Prayer and Worship

47. How do you pray?

That's a big question requiring a lifetime to explore. But I think the most basic truth about prayer is that we bring our praises, confessions, thanksgivings, and desires to God in the words we hear Him speaking to us in the Bible.

A child learns to talk to his parents by listening to his parents talk and repeating what they say. Jesus said in John 15:7, "If ye abide in me, and my words abide in you, ye shall ask what ye will, and it shall be done unto you." So our prayer life springs from God's Word as it dwells in us through faith in Christ.

For example, we hear God's Word tell us in Psalm 103:11, "For as the heaven is high above the earth, so great is his mercy toward them that fear him." So we pray, "Lord, I praise Thee for Thy love is big as the sky! How great is Thy mercy! Let me know it in my heart."

Or we hear His command in Exodus 20:12, "Honour thy father and thy mother: that thy days may be long upon the land which the LORD thy God giveth thee." So we pray, "God, please forgive me for disobeying my parents. I want to live a long and happy life. Please write Thy law upon my heart so that I will honor my father and my mother."

Or think of promises like Philippians 4:7, "And the peace of God, which passeth all understanding, shall keep your hearts and minds through Christ Jesus." So we pray, "God, I am anxious and worried today. Here is what I am fretting about. Please give me Thy peace, even when I don't understand what is happening in my life."

How do you pray? Read the Bible and use its words and ideas to pour out your heart to the Lord.

48. Do you think it's too simplistic to repeat the Lord's Prayer?

No, the Lord's Prayer is profound and full of truth. It is possible to repeat with words without understanding or without sincerity, which does us no good. But when prayed with meditation upon its meaning and a heart lifted up to God through Christ, the Lord's Prayer is a rich means of grace.

Consider the following meditation on the Lord's Prayer, based on writers from long ago:

Our Father: by right of creation, by generous provision, and by gracious adoption;

Which art in heaven: the throne of Thy glory, the temple of Thy angels, and the inheritance of Thy children;

Hallowed be Thy name: by the thoughts of our hearts, by the words of our mouths, and by the works of our hands;

Thy kingdom come: Thy kingdom of providence to defend us, of grace to conquer us, and of glory to crown us;

Thy will be done in earth, as it is in heaven: towards us without resistance, by us without being forced to, universally without exception, and eternally without backsliding;

Give us this day our daily bread: for the needs of our bodies, and for the eternal life of our souls;

And forgive us our debts: against the commands of Thy law, and against the grace of Thy gospel;

As we forgive our debtors: who sinned against us by hurting our reputation, by taking away our property, and by abusing our person;

And lead us not into temptation, but deliver us from evil: of overwhelming afflictions, of worldly enticements, of Satan's schemes, of false teaching's seductions, and of sinful desires.

For Thine is the kingdom, the power, and the glory forever: Thy kingdom ruling over all, Thy power conquering all, and Thy glory forever above all.

Amen: as it is in Thy purpose, and as it is in Thy promises, so it is in our prayers, and so it will be to Thy praise.

49. How many times have you prayed for something and didn't get it?

Many times. When we pray and pray but do not receive the answer we desire, it can be very painful. But that doesn't mean that it is a waste of time to pray or that you and I should stop praying. Unanswered prayer is an opportunity to grow in our faith and prayer life.

The main purpose of prayer is not to get answers, but to get God, that is, to glorify God and enjoy His presence. "O God, thou art my God; early will I seek thee: my soul thirsteth for thee" (Ps. 63:1). In other words, even if you don't receive an answer, you still must and ought to desire to pray. Do you know the joy of drawing near to God even if you don't feel or see an answer? "Trust in him at all times; ye people, pour out your heart before him: God is a refuge for us" (Ps. 62:8).

Ultimately, God is the answer to all our cries. Therefore we should pray more than anything for God to bless us and others with salvation and spiritual growth. This was Paul's great priority in prayer (Rom. 10:1; 15:13; Eph. 1:15-19; 3:14-21; Phil. 1:9-11; etc.).

As Jesus taught us, prayer at its core is developing your relationship with "our Father," seeking His glory, His kingdom, and His will before we seek our own needs. God is worthy of our prayers even if you don't receive an answer. We pray to Him to honor Him. We pray because He commands it; indeed he tells us to pray all the time (1 Thess. 5:17).

Keep asking God for things that seem good. The Father loves to give good gifts to His children (Matt. 7:9-11). If you feel like God is not answering your prayer, trust that His silence is a wise answer, framed by fatherly love.

Perhaps you are asking for something that would be bad for you. Perhaps you are seeking it with wrong motives and God's silence is to purify you (James 4:3). Maybe it's not the right time. It is God's will that we keep praying and not give up until God makes it clear that it's not His will (Luke 18:1-8).

Don't try to use prayer to make God follow your will. Use prayer to follow God's will. That's why we need always to pray: "*Thy* will be done" (Matt. 26:42). Oh, what a great blessing if we may truly pray this petition! Waiting on the Lord in a painful situation is incredibly hard. It's also amazingly helpful for our spiritual growth. "Wait on the LORD: be of good courage, and he shall strengthen thine heart: wait, I say, on the LORD" (Ps. 27:14). Pray on. Wait on. Hope on. You'll never be sorry.

50. What does the word "communion" mean?

Communion is sharing with friends. To commune with someone is like going over to a friend's house for dinner, conversation, and laughter (or tears). Let me highlight three ways the Bible speaks about communion.

First, we can have no spiritual communion with unbelievers (2 Cor. 6:14-17). In the unbeliever sin reigns, darkness snuffs out the light, Satan works freely, and idols are worshiped. In the believer righteousness reigns over the sin that remains, light is breaking into the darkness, Christ has conquered the devil, and God receives the praise.

That means that Christians cannot share in the worship or prayers of unbelievers. We should not attend the meetings of religions that do not preach the gospel of Christ. We can be friends with unbelievers and work alongside them at our school or job. But we must also be careful not to entangle ourselves in close relationships with them. We have no spiritual communion with the lost. "Can two walk together, except they be agreed?" (Amos 3:3). Instead we need to develop our closest friendships and most intimate sharing with godly people.

Second, we have communion with God. Paul wrote in 2 Corinthians 13:14, "The grace of the Lord Jesus Christ, and the love of God, and the communion of the Holy Ghost, be with you all. Amen." That means that the Holy Spirit brings us into a relationship of sharing life with the Father and the Son (1 John 1:3). God becomes our Father. Christ becomes our older Brother.

Therefore we should always be pursuing a deeper relationship with God through faith in Christ. Nothing is more exciting, fulfilling, and transforming than having God as your friend.

Nobody loves us like God does. Nothing is more noble and worthwhile than walking with God.

Third, we enjoy communion with God especially at the Lord's Supper. Paul said in 1 Corinthians 10:16, "The cup of blessing which we bless, is it not the communion of the blood of Christ? The bread which we break, is it not the communion of the body of Christ?" We call the Lord's Supper simply "Communion." By faith in Christ we eat a spiritual meal with our heavenly Friend, food He purchased by His death. We share this together as the family of God.

Christian children should think very highly of the Lord's Supper. Earnestly pursue a real faith in Christ, be bold to confess your faith before the church, and seek the church's blessing to join in Communion. For our communion is with Christ Himself.

51. What does the Apostles' Creed mean by "descended into hell," "quick," and "catholic"?

These three expressions in the creed can trip people up. Let me explain them.

In the creed we confess that we believe in Jesus Christ, God's Son, who "was crucified, dead and buried; He descended into hell." Some Christians have understood the Apostles' Creed to say that Christ visited hell after He died. However the Bible makes it clear that Christ's human spirit was in heaven the same day that He died (Luke 23:43, 46).

Reformed churches have taken "descended into hell" to mean that Christ suffered the equivalent of the pains of hell while on the cross (Gal. 3:13). He paid for our sins (Mark 10:45). The Heidelberg Catechism (Q. 44) says "that my Lord Jesus Christ, by His inexpressible anguish, pains, terrors, and hellish agonies, in which He was plunged during all His sufferings, but especially on the cross, hath delivered me from the anguish and torments of hell." This reminds us of how costly Christ's sacrifice was, and what an amazing salvation we have.

The Apostles' Creed also says that Christ "shall come to judge the quick and the dead." It is echoing Acts 10:42, where Peter said that after the Lord Jesus rose from the dead, "he commanded us to preach unto the people, and to testify that it is he which was ordained of God to be the Judge of quick and dead." Here "quick" does not mean fast or speedy. It has the old meaning of living or alive. When He returns in glory, He will judge everyone, both those who yet live and those who have died (2 Tim. 4:1; 1 Pet. 4:5). Are you ready for His return?

Later the creed states that we believe a "holy catholic church; the communion of saints." The word "catholic" does not refer to the Roman Catholic Church. The Pope did not rise up in power until centuries after this creed was written. Here "catholic" means universal, the church in all nations. And "communion of saints" means fellowship shared by everyone called by the gospel into a life of holiness by faith in Christ.

Do you believe these things? Have you been saved by Christ suffering God's wrath on the cross? When He returns, whether you are alive or dead, will His coming be a blessing or a curse for you? Are you a living part of the true church right now?

52. Do ministers have another job during the week? If not, what do they do with all their time?

Faithful pastors are very busy people. As the apostles said, "We will give ourselves continually to prayer, and to the ministry of the word" (Acts 6:4). They must study the Scriptures, and read good books about the Bible, theology, and people's lives. They must plan out how they will explain the Bible, give illustrations from ordinary life, and apply it to people. This is hard work, requiring many hours of labor. Good ministers are always learning from the Bible. Pastors must constantly be praying for God to give them understanding (Ps. 119:34, 36). They must pray without ceasing for God to enlighten the minds of their congregations (Eph. 1:19).

Ministers also have many other responsibilities. They must prepare for other parts of the worship services, such as baptism, the Lord's Supper, singing, and prayers. They must lead meetings of the elders, deacons, teachers, and congregations, and good leadership requires thoughtful preparation beforehand. They must teach catechism to children and classes to adults.

Pastors must visit the flock, for the very word "pastor" means shepherd and a shepherd must know his sheep (Prov. 27:23; John 10:3, 14, 27). They must speak the gospel to unbelievers, exhort lazy Christians, comfort the suffering, and rebuke the backslider. They must pray with the sick and elderly in their distresses. They must do pre-marital counseling and perform weddings for couples. When people come to them with problems, the minister must listen and offer wise advice. Ministers bear many burdens and carry many secrets.

Ministers must also seek to promote the gospel beyond their own congregations. They can evangelize the lost, write articles, blogs, and books, minister to churches without pastors, schools, nursing homes, jails, police, military personnel, represent the church in the community, promote good laws and public policies, cooperate with other ministers to plant new churches, and visit missionaries in other nations to encourage, pray, and preach.

Ministers have no lack of work to do. And we should not forget that they are mere men. They need to sleep, eat a healthy diet, exercise their bodies, spend time with their wives and children, go shopping, take a day off, care for their homes and yards, enjoy recreation, attend conferences and retreats, and go on vacations—just like everybody else. That's why it's so important for congregations to pay their pastors a good wage and support them wholeheartedly.

Most of all, pray for your ministers every day. Every pastor's cry is, "Pray for me!"

53. I got really sick and it still hurts to talk. Does that mean God doesn't want me to become a preacher?

Not necessarily. Don't assume that God doesn't want you to do something just because you have trouble with it right now. Wait upon the Lord. God may use your problem to get glory for Himself, just like the blind man whom Jesus healed (John 9:1-3).

Henry Bullinger was born in Switzerland in 1504. When he was a baby lots of people got sick and died from the plague. His family worried that he would die too, but he didn't. When he was a boy, he fell and was seriously wounded in his throat. He couldn't eat for five days. But again, God healed him. He went on to school in Prussia, and then to Cologne to study Greek and Latin. There he learned the gospel from books by men like Martin Luther. God worked in his heart, and he became a godly man.

Bullinger became a powerful preacher of the Word of God. He spent a lot of time studying the Bible and praying. He was very brave to speak against false teachers. He preached for forty years at Zurich. He wrote hundreds of books. His book of fifty sermons called the *Decades* was one of the best-selling books in England at the time.

Bullinger lived to be seventy-one years old. Though once so severely wounded in the throat he couldn't eat for days, his voice became a trumpet of God sounding forth the gospel.

So don't assume that sickness or an accident means that God is done with you. You might be surprised how much He does with your life. Be faithful to serve Him now as you can, and trust Him with the future.

Tough Questions About Other Religions

54. Why are there so many different religions? Are there many ways to God?

The Bible says, "God hath made man upright; but they have sought out many inventions" (Eccles. 7:29). When mankind fell into sin, we fell away from the true God and into idol worship and hatred against each other (Rom. 1:19-32). Our hearts became darkened and our thinking became very twisted and foolish (Eph. 4:17–18).

No longer knowing the true God, our hearts became idol factories, as Calvin said, making hundreds of gods out of anything we allowed to rule our hearts. So the human race became splintered and fragmented into many religions, fighting against each other and all against God.

Some people say that all the religions are different ways of seeking God. They say that we are like blind men feeling the parts of one elephant: one grasps the leg and thinks it is tree, another touches its side and thinks it is a wall, and a third feels its trunk and thinks it is a snake. They're all right, so we are told, and all have found the elephant. So all religions find God.

But that's nonsense. All the blind men were wrong: it wasn't a tree, or a wall, or a snake, but an elephant. If we believe that all religions reach the same God, then none of the religions are right. For they teach contradictory ideas. Hinduism worships millions of gods, and says we are all part of God. Islam teaches that God is absolutely one and cannot be a father to anyone. Christianity worships one God in three Persons: God the Father, God the Son, and God the Spirit. It also says that we are not God, but we can know God and become His children.

The Bible does not view the many religions of the world as many ways to God. Instead it says that Satan is the god of this world (2 Cor. 4:4). No one is truly seeking for God of his own initiative (Rom. 3:11). True religion is not man trying to find God, for man hates God.

True religion is God seeking man through Jesus Christ. Jesus said, "I am the way, the truth, and the life: no man cometh unto the Father, but by me" (John 14:6). Peter preached the name of Jesus Christ, saying, "Neither is there salvation in any other: for there is none other name under heaven given among men, whereby we must be saved" (Acts 4:12). We must know and trust and obey Jesus Christ, for apart from Him we can do nothing (John 15:5).

55. What's the difference between the Roman Catholic Church and the Reformed Church?

Of course, many people call themselves Catholic or Reformed but do not follow the teachings of those churches. We are talking about the official teachings of the churches, as found in their creeds, confessions, and catechisms. We might say that the key difference between these two religions is found in the words "alone" and "plus."

Reformed Christianity believes that our religious beliefs should come from *Scripture alone*. Faith comes by hearing the Word of God (Rom. 10:17), not the word of man (1 Thess. 2:13). Roman Catholicism teaches that religion comes from Scripture *plus* the church's traditions. Catholics must believe whatever the Pope teaches, even if it is not in the Bible.

Reformed Christianity believes that the mediator of salvation is *Christ alone*. He who redeemed us by His death on the cross is the only mediator between God and man (1 Tim. 2:5-6). Roman Catholicism teaches that Christ *plus* the Virgin Mary, angels, saints in heaven, and priests on earth are mediators of salvation from God to man. Therefore many Roman Catholics look to spirits in heaven and sacraments on earth (like baptism) to give them saving grace.

Reformed Christianity believes that God saves us by *grace alone*. We are dead in our sins and God must make us alive in Christ by a supernatural work (Eph. 2:1-5). Roman Catholicism teaches that God saves us by grace *plus* human effort. Salvation, they say, ultimately depends upon a person's free will, not God's loving purpose and power.

Reformed Christianity believes that God justifies us by *faith alone*. We must be justified as a free gift based upon Christ's obedience and death, received by faith or trust (Rom. 3:19-26).

God does not save us because of our works; we do good works because God saved us (Eph. 2:8-10). Roman Catholicism teaches that God justifies us by faith *plus* our works and merit. Catholics cannot be sure of their salvation and must constantly do deeds of penance.

Reformed Christianity believes that our salvation is for *the glory of God alone*. Since our salvation comes from the Father's eternal choice, was accomplished by Christ's redeeming death, and is applied by the Holy Spirit's sovereign power, it is totally to the praise of His glory (Eph. 1:3-14). God and only God should be worshiped (Matt. 4:10; Rev. 19:10). Roman Catholicism teaches that since the Virgin Mary and the saints have an important part in saving sinners, we should also give them a kind of worship as well.

I hope you can see that these are very serious differences.

56. Should a Christian go out on a date with a non-Christian?

No. Romantic friendship is not just short-term fun but a relationship designed to grow into lifelong companionship in marriage. Therefore we should never "go out," much less give our hugs and kisses and hearts to someone whom we could not see ourselves possibly marrying. To date or court a non-Christian is to form a special bond with them. Scripture says in 2 Corinthians 6:14, "Be ye not unequally yoked together with unbelievers: for what fellowship hath righteousness with unrighteousness? And what communion hath light with darkness?"

Dating a non-Christian exposes you to danger because they are not of the Lord. We must be careful of how our friendships may open us to potential harm. Jacob's daughter began spending time with the "daughters of the land," girls of pagan families. The next thing we hear about her is the sad news that she was raped by a pagan young man (Gen. 34:1-2).

Joining yourself to a non-Christian can break the hearts of your godly parents. Isaac's son Esau took Judith and Bashemath to be his wives. Both were from unbelieving people, and they "were a grief of mind unto Isaac and to Rebekah" (Gen. 26:35).

Dating a non-Christian can also bring sadness to future generations. Judah, a son of Jacob, became friends with an unbeliever named Hirah. When visiting him, Judah met a pagan girl named Shuah that he liked. He ended up marrying her. It was no surprise that when they had children, most of them grew up to be wicked in the sight of God. The Lord was so offended by Judah's children that He killed two of them (Gen. 38:1-10). Is that what you want?

Do you love Christ? If not, then you are not a Christian. If you do, then how can you join your life to someone who loves sin and hates Christ? For this reason, Paul said that if a Christian widow desires to marry again after her husband has died, "she is at liberty to be married to whom she will; only in the Lord" (I Cor. 7:39). Never develop a romantic friendship with someone who, as far as you can tell, is not in the Lord.

57. What is astrology? What does the Bible say about horoscopes?

Astrology is the ancient belief that the stars and planets influence our lives and destinies, together with a method of interpreting the motions of the stars to predict the future. Astrology is not the same as modern astronomy, which is the study of the stars, planets, and other objects in outer space according to the laws of science and mathematics.

Astronomy can honor the Creator because "the heavens declare the glory of God" (Ps. 19:1). Instead, astrology is a form of divination, trying to foretell the future based upon signs in the natural world.

If the stars control our lives, then they have divine power. We would then look to them for guidance and help. Therefore astrology directs our faith and worship to created things, which is idolatry.

The Bible strongly condemns worshiping the heavenly objects (Deut. 4:19; 17:2-5; 2 Kings 17:16; 21:5; 23:5). It also condemns divination, putting it in the same category as witchcraft (Deut. 18:9-14).

Reading a horoscope may seem innocent enough. But you are giving your mind over to superstition and looking to powers other than God to guide your life. Get rid of horoscopes and astrology books. Read the Bible. It reveals the God who created the stars and rules the life of every one of us. Know the Lord, and it will enrich you infinitely more than astrology ever could.

58. In 1 Samuel 28 Saul tried to contact a dead man's spirit. Did God really allow Samuel to talk to Saul, or is this Satan?

This is indeed a strange passage of Scripture. On the one hand, there is no indication anywhere else in the Bible that people can summon the spirits of the dead to speak to the living. All attempts at contacting spirits are strictly forbidden by the law (Deut. 18:10-11). Sorcerers will be cast into hell (Rev. 21:8). In Christ's story of the rich man and Lazarus, the rich man cannot leave hell to visit the earth and Abraham refuses to send the spirit of Lazarus back to warn the rich man's brothers, saying that they have the Scriptures (Luke 16:27-31).

However, 1 Samuel 28 does appear to say that Samuel's spirit came back from the dead to rebuke King Saul. The narrator of the text calls this apparition "Samuel" (1 Sam. 28:15-16). And his prophecy of the death of Saul and his sons came true.

However, it may be that the text also indicates that this is not what usually happens when people consult witches and spiritists. Verse 12 says, "And when the woman saw Samuel, she cried with a loud voice." This may suggest that this is not what she expected. Perhaps she was used to getting a demonic spirit, but not the spirit of a righteous man made perfect.

Paul writes elsewhere that those who participate in pagan worship have fellowship with demons (1 Cor. 10:20), and so we would expect that ordinarily those who try to contact spirits either connect to Satan and his demons, or the whole thing is a fake and a fraud. It may be that God did something unique here because Saul was the king of Israel, and his death would usher in the kingdom of David, the forefather of Christ.

So I would say that the spirit in 1 Samuel 28 appears to be Samuel, but that this was a very unusual occurrence for the spirits of the dead to converse with the living. The only other occurrence in Scripture which I can remember is when Moses and Elijah met with Jesus Christ on the mountain of His transfiguration, and they were not summoned by any sorcerer.

God absolutely forbids us to seek after the dead, but instead to follow the Scriptures (Isa. 8:19-20). When Saul sought the spirit of Samuel, even though he got Samuel, he also got a message of doom. That does not encourage us to seek to contact spirits!

59. Why do people go on suicide missions when suicide is wrong?

The Bible tells us that human life is precious because man is created in the image of God (Gen. 1:26; 9:6). The law of God forbids us to murder someone (Exod. 20:13). Many other religions also recognize that human life should be protected.

However, some groups have promoted the sad teaching that it is honorable to kill yourself if in the process you kill as many of your enemies as possible. In World War II a number of Japanese *kamikaze* pilots intentionally flew their planes into Allied ships. This expressed their devotion to the Shinto religion and their emperor, whom they worshiped as a god. The Tamil Tigers of Sri Lanka, of the Tamil people who are mostly Hindu, performed many suicide bombings in the late twentieth-century for political purposes.

Several Muslim groups teach that their god, Allah, will give a special place in paradise to suicide bombers. This is based on the Islamic concept of *jihad* or holy war and the violent example of Islam's chief prophet, Mohammed, and other leaders. Other Muslims argue that suicide attacks are wrong because life is sacred and should not be taken except by proper justice. But the sad fact remains that some Muslims continue to use violence and suicide attacks in hopes of destroying their enemies, advancing Islam, and gaining paradise.

Suicide bombings show us the power of false religious teachings. People by nature want to protect their lives. But false teachings can move people to throw away their lives to gain some reward. Suicide attacks are not ultimately a problem of race, politics, or money. They are a problem created by false teachings and false hope.

While our military must defend our nation against violent men, the greatest defense against such violence is to bring them the truth of Christ. But do we love Muslims and other people enough to do that? Do we pray for them? Or do we hate and fear them?

Christians went as missionaries to Japan after World War II, even though the Japanese killed many of our soldiers. Would we do the same for people of the Middle-East? True martyrdom is not killing yourself to kill others, but laying down your life to be a witness for Jesus Christ (Rev. 12:11).

Tough Questions About Hope and Eternity

60. I'm scared to die. Can God give me the strength to face death?

It is natural to fear death. Death is not the way God made the world to be. It is unnatural, an enemy, indeed a bitter result of sin. Yet Christ can give you the strength to face death boldly. Paul thought he might be put to death, yet believed that through the prayers of God's people "and the supply of the Spirit of Jesus Christ" he would be given boldness so that "Christ shall be magnified in my body, whether it be by life, or by death" (Phil. 1:19-20).

Godly men have wrestled with the fear of death. In the sixteenth century, Hugh Latimer was arrested and questioned until finally he signed a paper compromising his faith. But he repented of his compromise, and began to speak the Word of God boldly again.

Queen Mary then had Latimer and Nicholas Ridley arrested and imprisoned in the Tower of London. They were taken to be burned at the stake. When they came to the place of their execution, Ridley said, "Be of good cheer, brother Latimer, for God will either lessen the fury of the flames, or else strengthen us to bear them." When the wood beneath them was set on fire, Latimer said, "We shall this day light a candle, by God's grace, in England, as I trust shall never be put out."

Death can be a great struggle against fear, but the Lord is with us. Christ died to "deliver them who through fear of death were all their lifetime subject to bondage" (Heb. 2:15). For in His death for our sins Christ took away the sting of death, the wrath of God. Death will be painful for our bodies but need not terrify our souls, for we can be assured that because of Christ God will welcome us into heaven.

61. I heard someone talking about going to purgatory after you die. What's that?

The Roman Catholic Church teaches that Christians who die but are imperfectly purified of their sins must suffer in a cleansing fire. It claims to be able to grant indulgences which release souls from purgatory to go to heaven.

What a horrible idea! Christians who die go straight to heaven to be with Jesus Christ. He said to the repentant thief dying on the cross next to His, "Verily I say unto thee, Today shalt thou be with me in paradise" (Luke 23:43).

The moment a believer in Christ dies, the angels carry him into God's presence in heaven to be with the Lord and the spirits of righteous men and women who died before him (Luke 16:22; 2 Cor. 5:8). It is good to live and serve God on earth, but it is far better to die and be with Christ (Phil. 1:21-23).

The church does not have the authority to forgive sins. The church can only preach the promise of God that He forgives all who believe in Christ (Acts 10:43). Christ's blood washes us clean from all sin (1 John 1:7). His once-and-for-all sacrifice has completely and perfectly saved His people (Heb. 10:14). We cannot add or subtract from His perfect work of atonement. We can only rest our hearts in Him, trusting that Christ is enough to get us to heaven.

It is true that if we trust in Christ but are not very faithful, then we will lose rewards in heaven that we might have gained (Matt. 6:20; 1 Cor. 3:12-15). This should motivate us to serve the Lord with all our hearts. But the souls of godly Christians need not fear to die as if death takes them to more suffering. Death for them is the gateway into peace and rest from all their sorrows (Isa. 57:1-2). "Blessed are the dead which die in the Lord" (Rev. 14:13).

62. What happens to babies who die?

There is much that we do not know about these things, but the Bible teaches that: 1. All humans, even babies, are sinners in need of salvation (Ps. 51:5; 58:3). 2. Salvation is always through Christ (John 14:6). 3. God can work in babies so that they love Christ before they are born (Luke 1:39-44), though His ordinary way to save sinners is through His Word (Rom. 10:13, 17).

The Bible also indicates that believers can have the comfort that they will be reunited with their children who die in infancy. We read in 2 Samuel 12:23 that after David's child died, he said, "I shall go to him, but he shall not return to me."

This truth gave David comfort, enabled him to worship the Lord, and also helped him to comfort the child's mother. So he had a real hope of being with his child again, and so can we. Due to God's covenant faithfulness, we may trust that it is God's normal way to save babies of believers before they die.

The Lord has promised that His covenant faithfulness blesses not just believers but their children as well, reaching far ahead into future generations. Deuteronomy 7:9 says, "Know therefore that the LORD thy God, he is God, the faithful God, which keepeth covenant and mercy with them that love him and keep his commandments to a thousand generations."

We cannot assume that every child of a Christian will be saved. Each must be born again, or he will go the way of Esau, who went unrepentant into destruction though he had God-fearing Isaac for a father and Abraham for a grandfather. But it is God's ordinary way to bless the future generations of His covenant people, hearing their prayers for their children. Let us take comfort therefore in our covenant God.

63. Heaven seems a long time. Though I know it will be wonderful, won't we get bored? Eternity makes me slightly scared.

Eternity won't be boring, but a life of never-ending discoveries and pleasures. Ephesians 2:6-7 says, "And [God] hath raised us up together, and made us sit together in heavenly places in Christ Jesus: that in the ages to come he might shew the exceeding riches of his grace in his kindness toward us through Christ Jesus."

Each day in heaven, God will show us something more about his love for us. Since He has "exceeding riches" of grace, He will never run out of something new to reveal about His magnificent mercy, to the praise of His glorious grace. Furthermore, we will spend eternity reigning with the Lord as kings and queens in the new heaven and earth (Rev. 19–22). Sometimes this is described as living in a huge city of gold and gemstones. Cities are full of interesting things to do. They are places where people use their gifts in the arts and sciences and literature.

Sometimes the new creation is described like a wedding feast. Feasts are splendid gatherings of all kinds of people to talk to, a variety of delicious foods to eat, games, music, and entertainment. Imagine dining with Abraham and Sarah.

Sometimes the new creation is described like a garden. Gardens are lovely places to work and to explore. They have hundreds of varieties of flowers and butterflies. They require careful landscaping and cultivation. They may house sculptures and there are paths to hike, rivers, fountains, and waterfalls.

Best of all, every part of heaven will shine with the glory of God. We will be surrounded by His love and beauty. Eternity with an infinite Lover who is always showing us something new about His love for us—that doesn't sound boring to me!

64. What will we feel like in heaven if friends or family are not there with us?

Right now our natural affection goes out to our friends and family, and we long for all of them to be saved. Paul said in Romans 10:1, "Brethren, my heart's desire and prayer to God for Israel is, that they might be saved." It hurts to think that they might be condemned, and that's good that we feel that way (Rom. 9:2).

God's will has not yet been made clear, and so one day we may learn they have been saved. But after the resurrection, all our affections will flame with holiness and delight in God's will. We will then hate sin with all that we are. Our whole mindset will be very different than it is now.

And it will be clear on Judgment Day whom God has condemned for their sins and whom God has saved by His grace. So we will rejoice in God's judgment of the wicked, even if some of them were once our friends or family. If they go to the grave refusing to repent, then they will prove not to be true friends or family after all. We will have a new family in Christ.

On that day the saints will worship God for His judgments on the wicked, saying, "Even so, Lord God Almighty, true and righteous are thy judgments," and "Alleluia; Salvation, and glory, and honour, and power, unto the Lord our God: for true and righteous are his judgments" (Rev. 16:7; 19:1-2).

65. When people die in an explosion their bodies are torn to pieces. How will they be raised from the dead?

The resurrection of everyone will be a miracle. It's not just about explosions and crashes. A person's flesh naturally dissolves into dirt within about a year of death, and after centuries not even the bones may be left. The bodies of those who died thousands of years ago are gone without a trace unless preserved by special conditions.

Christ's work of raising the dead will be a work of such power that only God could do it (John 5:21). He will use that same power to resurrect people as He uses to bring all the universe under His Lordship (Phil. 3:21). God knows everything and keeps track of the tiniest parts of our bodies: "the very hairs of your head are all numbered" (Matt. 10:30). He rules over the whole natural world (Ps. 104). The Lord is able to do anything He pleases to do (Ps. 135:6).

Our attitude to the Lord should always be, "Lord, if Thou art willing, Thou art able" (see Matt. 8:2). We know that God is willing to do what He has promised to do. The resurrection of the dead is a plain promise of Scripture. It was predicted by the prophets (Dan. 12:13) and proclaimed by the apostles (1 Cor. 15).

The resurrection was promised by Christ: "Marvel not at this: for the hour is coming, in the which all that are in the graves shall hear his voice, and shall come forth; they that have done good, unto the resurrection of life; and they that have done evil, unto the resurrection of damnation" (John 5:28-29).

Do you believe that Christ is the almighty God? If we doubt the resurrection because we can't understand how God will do it, then, like the Sadducees, we have made the mistake of knowing neither the Scriptures, nor the power of God (Matt. 22:29).

66. If our sins are the same and nobody is better than another does everybody get the same penalty in hell?

When we say that no one is better than anybody else, you need to understand what we mean. No one is better *by nature*, for apart from God's grace we are all dead in sin and objects of God's wrath (Eph. 2:1-3). No one is better *in spiritual ability* because no one is able to submit to God's law or come to Christ (Rom. 8:7; John 6:65). Furthermore, no one is better *in merit* because all sins deserve the fires of hell, even insulting words or lustful thoughts (Matt. 5:22, 28-29). No one deserves to go to heaven except Jesus Christ.

However, that does not mean that all sins are equally bad in every respect or that all persons deserve the exact same punishment from God. It is bad to covet money, but worse to rob a bank and take away the savings of hundreds of people. It offends God if you hate someone, but it is worse if you murder him and send his family into a tailspin of bereavement and loss.

God will send worse punishments on some sinners than others. Christ actually said that it would be better on Judgment Day for the cursed city of Sodom than it will be for some people (Matt. 10:15; 11:24). Christ warned that those who have more knowledge of His commandments will be punished more severely than ignorant sinners (Luke 12:47-48).

Everyone in hell will desperately wish they had committed even one less sin, for they will long for the slightest relief from their agony, a drop of water to cool their tongue in the fire. But it will be denied them. Now is the time for repentance, and if we don't listen to the Bible now, even someone rising from the dead could not convince us to repent (Luke 16:25-31).

67. What is hell like?

The Lord Jesus said, "And if thine eye offend thee, pluck it out: it is better for thee to enter into the kingdom of God with one eye, than having two eyes to be cast into hell fire: where their worm dieth not, and the fire is not quenched" (Mark 9:47-48). He is not telling you to cut out your eyes. Your eyes are not the problem; sin comes from the heart. He was using strong words to tell us how serious hell is and how important it is to repent of our sins.

From Christ's words we see several things about hell.

Hell is worse than any pain or problem on earth. Having an eye or hand or foot cut off would be horrible, but it's nothing compared to hell (Mark 9:43, 45, 47).

Hell means God shuts us out from His kingdom. It's like being thrown out of a party where there is delicious food, good friends, and lots of fun, and being sent away into a place of terrifying darkness where you weep and grind your teeth in frustration (Matt. 22:12-13).

Hell is a punishment forced on sinners, not their own desire. People choose to reject God of their own will, but Christ said they will be "cast" or "thrown" there (Mark 9:47; Matt. 5:30). I remember a girl from high school who boasted that if she went to hell at least she would not be alone there. She died a year later of a brain tumor. People who boast about going to hell do not know what they are talking about.

Hell is the painful burning of God's wrath against sinners. Christ compared it to "fire." It's not just separation from all that is good. It is unbearable pain. "Who among us shall dwell with the devouring fire? Who among us shall dwell with everlasting burnings?" (Isa. 33:14). For it is produced by the righteous anger of the all-powerful God (Deut. 32:22; Rev. 14:10).

Hell is like constantly dying alone. When Christ said, "their worm dieth not," He spoke of an experience of death and decay that would never end. Christ also compared hell to darkness (Matt. 25:30), and darkness isolates you from others. Once I went into a hospital where two women lay dying. Both groaned in pain, unable to hear each other. The room could have been filled with people, but they felt completely alone. "Oh," I thought, "this is a little bit of what hell will be like—always dying, but never dead; always surrounded by others, yet fully alone."

Hell is forever. "The fire is not quenched." It is "everlasting punishment" (Matt. 25:46). The Bible warns that "the smoke of their torment ascendeth up for ever and ever: and they have no rest day nor night" (Rev. 14:11). Once you go there you cannot get out. But you can avoid going to hell because Christ has suffered hell for sinners on the cross. Trust in Christ alone for salvation!

68. What will be the best part of heaven?

There will be many good things about heaven: seeing old friends, making new friends, and living without temptation, sin, pain, or death.

But there is one thing that will make heaven truly heaven: the glory of God in Christ. Jesus prayed for this out of His love for His friends, "Father, I will that they also, whom thou hast given me, be with me where I am; that they may behold my glory" (John 17:24).

The Book of Revelation says it very sweetly when it declares, "And the city had no need of the sun, neither of the moon, to shine in it: for the glory of God did lighten it, and the Lamb is the light thereof" (Rev. 21:23). We shall see His face, and that will be everything to us.

John Owen was dying in the year 1683 after a lifetime of studying the Bible, keeping its commands, preaching, and writing. He was one of the greatest theologians the world has ever known. He had spent many years meditating on how beautiful Christ is, and communing with Him in the Holy Spirit.

As he was dying, a friend came to tell him that his book, *The Glory of Christ,* was at the presses to be printed. Owen replied, "I am glad, but the long looked for day for is come at last in which I shall see that glory in another manner than I have ever done yet, or was capable of doing in this world!"

It is precisely this that led Paul to say, "To live is Christ, and to die is gain" (Phil. 1:21). May the Lord help you to say the same, to live the same, and when you die, to discover the same.

Books by Joel R. Beeke and Diana Kleyn

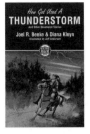

How God Used a Thunderstorm
ISBN: 978-1-85792-815-0

The mountains are dark and looming as the lightening splits across the sky. The forest offers shelter and in the distance the traveller spots a lamp. Rushing towards the door he doesn't realise that someone has planned this journey - there is a woman in the house who needs to hear about her loving Savior, Jesus Christ. God has sent the traveller to tell her about himself.

How God Used a Snowdrift
ISBN: 978-1-85792-817-4

A hostile army is rapidly approaching the little Baltic village. Karl and his mother are in fear of their lives. Karl barricades the door to the cottage but his mother reads the Bible. In the end God uses a snowdrift to protect them from the enemy. So how does He do that? Find out by reading the rest of the story and there are lots of other stories in this book too.

How God Stopped the Pirates
ISBN: 978-1-85792-816-7

As the pirates near the helpless ship they raise their grappling irons and prime their cannons for battle. The captain stands ready to defend his vessel and the lives of the people on board. The missionaries go to their cabins to pray. Can anyone stop these pirates? God can. There are lots of stories in this book. Read about the pirates, a burglar and a Russian servant girl as well as many other stories about the amazing things that missionaries get up to as well as how God can change lives.

How God Sent a Dog to Save a Family

ISBN: 978-1-85792-819-8

Emma and Alex have had nothing to eat all day and there is no food in the kitchen or the store cupboard. Their mother has no money to buy food and all that she can do is pray that somehow, someone will send them something to eat. But in the morning something is scratching at the door and the children go out to investigate. Find out who or what it is and discover how God has answered the families' prayers. Read other stories too about flying bread, Martha's Raven and the Stolen Sleigh. You will find out about how God cares for us and about how children can believe in him.

How God Used a Drought and an Umbrella

ISBN: 978-1-85792-818-1

It was the longest drought that anyone in the county had ever seen. Everyone was praying for rain. The fields were dry, the animals were thirsty and everyone was really hot. But only one little girl really believed that God would answer and she taught her minister a lesson. Find out how she did this by reading the rest of the story and others in this book. Read about the drought, the poor man who was made rich and the shepherd boy who lost his sheep. You will also read about people and lots of children who faithfully stood up for Jesus.

TRUTHFORLIFE®

THE BIBLE-TEACHING MINISTRY OF **ALISTAIR BEGG**

The mission of Truth For Life is to teach the Bible with clarity and relevance so that unbelievers will be converted, believers will be established, and local churches will be strengthened.

Daily Program

Each day, Truth For Life distributes the Bible teaching of Alistair Begg across the U.S., in selected cities in Canada, and in several locations outside of the U.S. on over 1,700 radio outlets. To find a radio station near you, visit **truthforlife. org/station-finder.**

Free Teaching

The daily program, and Truth For Life's entire teaching archive of over 2,000 Bible-teaching messages, can be accessed for free online and through Truth For Life's full-feature mobile app. A daily app is also available that provides direct access to the daily message and daily devotional. Download the free mobile apps at **truthforlife.org/app** and listen free online at **truthforlife.org.**

At-Cost Resources

Books and full-length teaching from Alistair Begg on CD, DVD and MP3CD are available for purchase *at cost, with no mark up*. Visit **truthforlife.org/store.**

Where To Begin?

If you're new to Truth For Life and would like to know where to begin listening and learning, find starting point suggestions at **truthforlife.org/firststep.** For a full list of ways to connect with Truth For Life, visit **truthforlife.org/subscribe.**

Contact Truth For Life

P.O. Box 398000 Cleveland, Ohio 44139
phone 1 (888) 588-7884   **email** letters@truthforlife.org
 /truthforlife   @truthforlife truthforlife.org